I'VE STILL GOT ME

A Widow's Journey to Love, Happiness, and Financial Independence

Michelle P. Cooper

Copyright © 2018 Michelle P. Cooper

All rights reserved. This book or any portion thereof may not be reproduced or used in any manner whatsoever without the express written permission of the author except for the use of brief quotations in a book review.

To my strong mother, who planted my seed of independence and my caring father, who has been there for me through thick and thin. To my loving husbands past and present for making my life as amazing as it is today, and for my children—Alec, Chloe, Gillian, Daniel and Alex—whom I love more than they will ever know.

Table of Contents

LETTER TO MY READERS

1	THE LAST PHONE CALL	3
2	"CAN I KEEP THE HOUSE?"	21
3	SHOW ME THE MONEY! HOW AM I PAYING FOR ALL OF THIS?	42
4	ESTATE PLANNING BASICS—WHAT IF SOMETHING HAPPENS TO ME?	60
5	MOMMY GUILT	91
6	FINDING LOVE AGAIN—IS IT POSSIBLE?	107
7	IT'S COMPLICATED—BLENDING YOUR FAMILY WITH LOVE	123
8	KIDS AND MONEY	142
9	ELDERCARE—THE BEST IS YET TO COME	164

A CLOSING NOTE PUTTING IT ALL TOGETHER, TAKING ACTION, AND EMPOWERING OURSELVES — 180

APPENDIX — 182

ONE MORE THING! — 197

Letter to My Readers

When I was 36, my husband killed himself. Our twins were toddlers. On top of managing my overwhelming grief, I had to figure out our finances and see if we could keep our house.

That time was indescribably difficult. Yet I had advantages a lot of women don't—a law background, a business degree, and work experience in estate planning, which led my husband and me to be mostly prepared. We had savings, a financial advisor, life insurance, and other parts in place for our financial security. But still, I struggled to wrap my arms around the financial tasks my husband had once handled.

You see, Scott and I fell into the typical male-female roles. He handled investing. I handled "everything children." I oversaw finances and numbers all day at work, so I was happy to leave our personal investments and day-to-day expenses to Scott. He loved it. On top of these self-assigned roles, we had demanding careers.

In my daily work, I help couples plan their estates, and it works best when both partners are active participants.

Again and again, I see what happens to women who haven't taken an active role in their finances and estate planning. Women going through life transitions seek my help. Sometimes, women at retirement age return to work, because they haven't saved enough money to sustain their current lifestyle and have not prepared for a worst case scenario. Sometimes they are forced to sell their houses.

This book represents my passion to help you plan a great life. You might be wondering if you will be okay in 20 or 30 years. You might be newly widowed or divorced and wondering if you can continue living the lifestyle you've been enjoying. You might be wanting to plan ahead to feel more comfortable and secure but not know what to do next.

I can tell you that I've been there, and in this book, I share my personal journey and the steps to take to be in control of your financial future.

I've helped hundreds of women plan better futures. I have learned the power that comes with financial knowledge and financial security. I have learned that I can draw on my unique blend of knowledge and skills—legal and financial experience, widowhood, and loss of loved ones—to guide you in creating a healthy future.

It's taken me 13 years to put pen to paper (or fingers to keyboard) to write this book, because I was not comfortable sharing my story for a long time. I felt self-conscious about the circumstances around my husband's death. But I knew I had to overcome that and share my story as a wake-up call to other women who assume their futures will be financially secure no matter what happens.

As women, we face several of the same challenges. Many of us are constantly juggling the demands of being a good wife, mother, employee, daughter, and friend. We typically do this without putting ourselves first, but this paradigm needs to change. Chances are that we will need to rely on ourselves at some point in our lives.

Women typically live longer than men, and statistics show that we earn less than they do. Although studies show that a woman's confidence in her financial abilities is less than her male counterpart, she does better than her male counterpart when she takes a role in her financial life. In order to be empowered and independent financially, we all need to take an active role in our financial well-being. The good news is that it can be done, and all it takes is the willingness to do it. I am living proof of that. You, too, can accomplish this by being proactive, starting early, and following a plan—whether you are single, married, widowed, or divorced.

I'VE STILL GOT ME

A Widow's Journey to Love, Happiness,
and Financial Independence

1

The Last Phone Call

> "Life changes fast. Life changes in the instant. You sit down to dinner and life as you know it ends."
> –Joan Didion, *The Year of Magical Thinking*

My husband, Scott, disappeared on March 28, 2005. In the weeks afterward, I could have been a chair at our kitchen table. I spent hours there thinking about where he could be and what I could do to find him faster. In the hopes of expediting the search for him, I'd shared my husband's story with a *Washington Post* reporter.

The reporter, along with my father and brother, was sitting at the kitchen table with me when I first learned what had become of Scott.

"It's the police," my brother said, handing me the phone.

The police told me that kayakers on the Potomac River found Scott's body, and they wanted me to confirm it was him.

I'VE STILL GOT ME

Lately, I'd been feeling like my life resembled a TV drama. What was happening—missing husband, search dogs, police interviews, news reporters—didn't feel real. After I hung up the phone, I returned to the table and told everyone what the police had said.

At first, no one spoke.

The reporter broke the silence. "Is there anything you want to say?" he asked.

Although Scott had disappeared weeks earlier, it wasn't until that call that I knew for certain he wasn't coming back. I was in shock. Originally, the reporter planned to write about my husband's disappearance. After that phone call, the story turned into an article about what happened. I felt grief-stricken, and I'd not eaten a normal meal in days. But I was the sole parent of twins now, and I would have to figure out my life without him.

Although my husband had called me before he took his life, he hadn't left me a note or any explanation of why he did it. I'd wrestle with that question for years. My last conversation with Scott happened the afternoon he disappeared. He was talking to me, and then, at some point later that day, he was gone.

The Last Phone Call

SCOTT WAS TALL, athletic and clean cut. He prided himself on doing the right thing and following rules. He was also a hard worker and put himself through undergrad at The University of Virginia and then Medical School at SUNY Syracuse. His training was in Physiatry (Physical Medicine and Rehabilitation), but he had switched to Phlebology (the treatment of varicose veins) a couple of years prior. Although he loved his new specialty, he recently had a parting of ways with his employer and decided to start his own vein institute.

When Scott called me that day, I was sitting at my desk. I'd been gazing at the top of the National Cathedral in Washington, DC, and feeling appreciative of the sight despite the day's cloudy, wet weather. My top-floor view from a spacious suite and my office's location in DC's business epicenter reminded me that I had "made it."

I smiled at how far I'd come—*we'd* come. Scott and I had married in 1997, and the previous eight years meant living in California and Maryland, accepting new jobs or promotions, and having two children. We'd moved into our recently built "forever house" after choosing custom tilework and finishes for the interior. We'd worked hard and stuck together, and it had paid off in happiness and satisfaction for both of us—or so I'd thought.

When the phone rang, I knew it was Scott on the phone. He called every day in the late afternoon to ask how my day was going. We'd talk about what to have for dinner and decide who would get home first to relieve the sitter. I looked forward to these daily check-in calls and the opportunity to connect with my husband. I loved having a partner to share my life with—whether we spoke for one minute or thirty.

That day, our conversation seemed strange. But I didn't notice that until later—too late, I realize now.

"Hello honey, how is your day going?" I waited for Scott's reply and our normal banter to begin. But it didn't.

I only heard silence.

"Scott, are you there?"

"Michelle, I love you," he replied. His words sounded slurry and distorted. But the words were nice to hear, and I loved his over-the-phone hug.

"Scott, I love you, too. How is your day going? What do you want to make for dinner tonight?" I straightened the papers on my desk.

"I love you Michelle…I love you Michelle," he said.

"I love you, too, Scott. Let's figure out what we're making for dinner, so I know if I need to pick up something from the store on my way home." I wanted to write out my evening to-do list and add any needed groceries to it.

The Last Phone Call

He didn't offer a good or clear response when I asked where he was, but I didn't think much of it at the time. He was probably at work or heading home. As usual, I was in my business mode, which meant I was listening to our conversation while multi-tasking. I wanted to make sure my work was in order as I closed up shop for the day. He didn't say much more than that he loved me. Since I wanted to finish up at work and head home to him and our twins, I cut the conversation short and said I loved him and would see him at home.

In the silence of the parking garage elevators, my mind turned back to the telephone call with Scott. I began to mull over and dissect our conversation the way our brains do when we have a quiet moment. My heart began to race. The conversation we'd had wasn't normal. We hadn't had our usual back-and-forth banter, and he'd kept repeating how much he loved me. Something wasn't right.

I dialed Scott's cell number. I wanted to hear his voice again and to ask him what was wrong. No answer.

With one hand on the steering wheel, I kept pressing redial on my cell phone for the next 30 minutes. Each time I got his voicemail, I left a message asking him to call me back. I pleaded. No luck.

Maybe his office would know something. I called his office and spoke with the nurse who worked with him. She told me he had left hours ago, which added to my uneasiness. If Scott had left hours ago, where was he, and why was he not picking up his phone now?

Desperate to speak with someone for reassurance, I called my dad, who was close to both of us. Thankfully, he answered right away. I told him about my odd conversation with Scott. I expressed dread that something was not right with his tone of voice and speech, recounted every word of our conversation, and shared that I'd not been able to get Scott on the phone ever since. In his usual calm manner, my dad told me not to worry and to keep driving home. He said Scott was probably running an errand, seeing a patient, or at home waiting for me.

"Okay," I said. But I still felt panic, and I couldn't help but wonder if my dad was putting on a brave front. He knew Scott well and knew this was unusual.

I hurried home through Washington's notoriously bad rush hour traffic. I thought if I could just get home, I might find Scott in our kitchen.

Usually, when I returned home, I felt excited to see the kids and Scott. But today, I felt apprehension and fear. When I opened the garage door to the kitchen, the twins ran up to greet me. From our home's garage entrance, we walked straight into the kitchen, where the kids spent a lot

The Last Phone Call

of time with their spongy play mats, blocks, and bouncy seats. They'd play there while the sitter prepped dinner.

That day, I entered the kitchen, thinking, "I hope Scott's here." He wasn't in the kitchen, but maybe he was elsewhere.

"Hi. Is Scott home?" I asked the sitter.

"Nope," she replied.

Only the sitter was there with the children, and she had no idea what I was about to tell her.

My panic increased. I had a feeling something bad had happened.

The past few months had been challenging for us. Although Scott's new vein practice was going well, his job loss affected and challenged us both. As an optimist and the cheerleader in our marriage, I had the mindset that life is full of challenges, and we'd face them all together. In a marriage, we think we know the minds of our spouses. We think we're sharing everything, yet I discovered my optimistic view of our situation differed from Scott's.

With my sitter wanting to leave for the day and my two-year-old twins wanting more cuddles and attention, I grabbed the telephone and called Scott again. No answer. I left yet another voicemail begging him to call me back—I'd lost track of how many I'd left—no matter what was happening. I desperately needed to hear his voice and know that he was okay.

The sitter left, and the twins held onto my legs. I'd need to figure out what to feed them and how I'd put them to bed. But first, I called my dad to say Scott wasn't home, even though it was later than his normal arrival time. My dad told me not to worry and that Scott would be home soon. Afterward, I called my brother. I told him the same story about the conversation I'd told my dad and how I knew something wasn't right. He reassured me that Scott would be home soon.

Scott never returned home. By 8:00 p.m., dread washed over me. No one could tell me Scott's location, and every call I made to his cell phone dumped me straight into voicemail. Both my dad and brother had come over to help me figure out what to do next. I waited before calling Scott's parents. I didn't want to worry them unless something was really wrong. As the night wore on, we decided to call the police and file a missing person's report. Scott was a reliable person. It was out of character for him to be gone like this.

The police arrived, and we sat at the kitchen table. Although I was nervous to talk with them, I was hopeful that they could locate Scott and end this nightmare. They asked me questions, and I gave them all the information I had.

The Last Phone Call

After the police left, my dad helped me get the twins bathed and ready for bed. The two toddlers were running in different directions. My son Alec hit his head on the side of the dresser and cut himself. Meanwhile, Chloe was teetering on the futon chair in her room and about to fall off. I wondered if the kids could sense this wasn't a normal night. They didn't want to go to bed, and they both wanted my immediate and undivided attention. I realized that, if Scott didn't return, I'd be left caring for my two two-year-olds alone. I wondered how I would handle both children by myself on top of everything else going on. In a complete fog, I muddled through bath and story time and got the kids to sleep.

I pleaded with my dad to stay over that night. He did. I didn't want to be alone. For the first time in my life, I was in a state of complete despair with no rational idea of how to solve the problem. Normally, I think creatively and solve problems no matter what challenge presents itself. That night, I could not come up with any solutions. A gnawing feeling in the pit of my stomach told me that I was alone and that my wonderful life as part of a married couple might be over.

I didn't sleep a minute. For the rest of my life, I'll remember the raw emotions of fear, panic, and dread that pulsed through me. I couldn't comprehend how I got to this place of panic and terror. My life had been so normal, hopeful, and full of goodness—as recently as that morning.

The kids woke up at 6:00 a.m. the next day. I desperately wanted this morning to be like other mornings, but Scott was gone and my dad was there. This already wasn't like other mornings. Scott and I had our routines down pat. We'd wake up ourselves, tag team with waking the twins up, feed the children, and get ourselves ready for work while the twins played in our bedroom. We worked well as a team. So on this morning, I felt like a limb was missing. I felt I couldn't cope with the twins, my day, and the rest of my life.

I felt appreciative that my dad had spent the night at my house the night before. We were close throughout my childhood and especially after my mother passed away from ovarian cancer when I was in my mid-twenties. I've always looked up to him. He was close with Scott and knew something wasn't right when Scott didn't come home the night before. Even though my dad was putting up a good front, I could sense that he was extremely worried.

I decided it was time to call Scott's parents. By the time I called them, I was so desperate for answers that I immediately broke into tears when I heard my mother-in-law's voice. After I explained what had happened, his parents became concerned and worried. We all knew Scott

The Last Phone Call

was reliable and responsible, and this situation was out of the ordinary. You could count on Scott. In fact, his reliability appealed to me the most when we were dating. I had looked for a husband that I felt I could count on in sickness and in health—just like my mother had counted on my father to support her through her battle with cancer.

How ironic, I thought, that the current situation was directly counter to Scott's reliable nature. I had thought I could count on Scott for the rest of my life. We'd tried for years to have children, and he'd been supportive through every step. Scott helped me through the emotional roller coaster of in vitro fertilizations, and he attended to my every need when I was on bed rest. Our twins arrived early, and Scott was by our sides during the birth, my stay in the hospital, and the resulting sleepless nights. The first two years of Alec and Chloe's lives were two of the most special of my life. I had the husband, the family, and the career I had always wanted. We had love, a beautiful home, a close and supportive family, and shared values. But Scott wasn't here for any of that now, and I could not make sense of it.

Over the next two and a half weeks, one day melted into the next. I had no direction. I existed only to care for my children, and they needed me more than ever. I couldn't eat or sleep, and I couldn't think clearly. By this time, I'd shared my situation with friends, colleagues, and the news media.

I sought any help possible to find my husband, so we could return to our regular life. I became more depressed. Friends and colleagues stopped by to help me create flyers to post around town. The evening news featured our story, and I began to have that feeling again that my life was one of those TV shows I watched on sick days. Tissues in hand, I would become emotionally ensnared in a gut-wrenching story on the TV while home sick in bed, except now that story was my life.

My days became a blur of activities related to Scott's disappearance. I called *The Washington Post* to ask for their help in finding Scott. When the reporter interviewed me, the words rolled off my tongue. I'd told the story so many times by that point. A work colleague, who volunteered as a firefighter, took it upon himself to make solving this case his mission. Daily, and multiple times a day, I called Scott's parents to give them updates. During one of these conversations, Scott's father mentioned to me that it might be a good idea to search for Scott near water. I was not sure what he meant, but a telephone call from the police supported my father-in-law's suggestion.

At about 3:00 a.m. one morning, a detective called to ask if they could come over and get some of Scott's personal belongings. Bleary eyed and dazed, I welcomed them to my house to get the items. They took Scott's hairbrush and one

The Last Phone Call

of his shoes. An officer had found Scott's abandoned car on River Road, which borders the Potomac River. Scott and I frequently drove on River Road to get to the C&O Canal, where we would hike and take the twins for rides in their jogging stroller.

The police explained they had enlisted the help of trained dogs. The personal items would allow the dogs to identify Scott's scent, find it in the grass, and follow it. In law school, I didn't enjoy criminal law, and I was not a fan of reading crime novels. I had no interest in solving mysteries as a pastime. All I wanted now was for my life to return to normal. After the police left with Scott's personal belongings, I could not fall back to sleep despite taking sleeping pills.

I hadn't left my house in days. I still couldn't eat. Several hours later, the police called. The dogs had traced Scott's scent to a neatly folded pile of clothes in the woods near the bank of the C&O Canal. Scott had driven all the way up River Road, parked his car, consumed an entire bottle of Tylenol PM with water, and walked one mile toward the C&O Canal. The empty Tylenol PM bottle and water were found, along with his keys, on the floor of his car. The wallet Scott had left inside his folded pants allowed the police to conclude this pile of clothing had belonged to him.

Despite this news, I had hopes that Scott was alive somewhere in the woods. I wanted to find him no matter what condition he might be in. Washington, DC, has unpredictable weather, and this early spring had been gloomy and cold. With the new police report, I imagined Scott alone in the woods, shaking and cold, clinging to a branch for support. If only they could find him soon.

My hopes didn't last long. The police told me the dogs picked up Scott's scent on the other side of the canal. They suggested that my husband walked one mile under the influence of Tylenol PM, took his clothes off, trudged through several feet of swampy canal water, and waded to his eventual death in the Potomac River. At the same time, my hopes were decimated; I refused to believe any of this had happened to my husband. If you asked me how I could possibly believe the sad truth and hope he was alive at the same time, I could only tell you that such thinking is the work of shock and grief on the human brain.

Scott was a competitive swimmer, an experienced scuba diver, and enjoyed swimming with sharks. I couldn't believe Scott could or would allow himself to drown. In fact, it seemed crazy to me. Days passed with no more answers. I kept asking myself, "Why?" Why would Scott do such a thing?

The Last Phone Call

As if the grief and despair wasn't enough to handle, the police called me in to question me as a suspect. I was naïve and had no idea about their intentions. I asked my firefighter friend to come with me for support. I had hopes that the conversation with the police would help me find Scott. I was completely wrong. Other than getting car seats installed before the twins were born, I had never visited a police station. I felt frail and weak from lack of food and sleep and, through the questioning, learned I was considered a suspect in my husband's disappearance. As tears streamed down my face, the detective asked me why there were so many dropped telephone calls the day Scott disappeared. I repeated the same answer again and again.

"I was trying to get him to pick up the telephone," I said. I could barely choke out the words, because I was crying so hard.

I recounted our strange conversation to the detective. He wasn't buying it. He was trying to force me to give him an answer that was different than the truth, so he could close this case. I was shaking and sobbing, and I was grateful to have a friend waiting for me outside. Afterward, I felt I'd been beaten up in a boxing match. I could not have felt more drained, devastated, and weak. My normally strong exterior was wiped out. I had nothing left to give at this point, and the officer finally let me go. In hindsight, I see how naïve I was not to realize that a spouse is always a suspect in a case like this.

After nearly two weeks, we began to lose hope of ever finding Scott's body. I spoke with my Rabbi and asked him for guidance. Together with my dad and Scott's parents, we all decided that I needed closure. I could not continue living each day at my kitchen table waiting for the telephone to ring. I needed to forge a new path for my life, and that life was most likely not going to be with Scott. We decided it would be best to start planning Scott's funeral. I had pretty much accepted that Scott was not returning to our home or to his role as my husband or as father to our children. From our synagogue, I purchased two burial plots next to each other and near my mother's resting place. Since we'd not found Scott's body, I called the cemetery and arranged to have a memorial service. I did not want to succumb to the finality of a funeral—what if he returned?—but friends and family advised me that I had to have a service in order to move on with my life.

I made the memorial service arrangements the night *The Washington Post* reporter sat at my kitchen table. He'd planned to finish his article about the disappearance and had some follow-up questions before the newspaper published the story. When the police called to tell us Scott had been found, the story of disappearance became a story about suicide.

When the police called, they asked for a description of Scott's personal effects. I described Scott's blue Tag Heuer Submariner watch and platinum wedding band with gold trim. They confirmed the person they'd found was him. Now we knew for certain. I felt a combination of feelings when they told me they'd finally found Scott—deep sadness and relief. Although the mystery of Scott's disappearance was solved, it meant my future life without Scott was now a reality with all of its attached grief and uncertainty.

The memorial service arrangements turned into funeral arrangements. I spent hours reaching out to everyone I knew who had touched Scott's life in some way. I wanted those who were part of our lives to have the chance to say goodbye to him. I wanted to look back at this time and be proud I'd done the right thing. Yet, as much as I wanted to have a proper funeral for Scott, I dreaded it. Many of the details from that day are wiped out of my memory. Thankfully, our brains have a way of protecting us from the details of traumatic situations. However, I do remember I reluctantly walked up to Scott's casket and put my arms around it. This was my first and last opportunity to say goodbye to the man I loved. That moment marked for me both the end of my innocence and the start of my life as a widow and single mother of two.

Over 150 people attended Scott's funeral. After the funeral, we held Shiva at our (now "my") house for the next seven days. Over 100 people filled our house afterward. With the mirrors covered and the countertops filled with food, I felt like I was floating on the outskirts of a party I didn't want to attend. Usually, I loved to entertain. In an everyday situation, I'd enjoy planning the guest list, menu, flowers, and table settings. Most of all, I loved when guests came together in our home and had a great time. Again, I felt conflicting feelings at the Shiva. I didn't want to be alone, yet I also didn't want to be at the center of all this attention.

Our kitchen counters were large, and they held food platters, photos of Scott and family, and a Shiva candle from the synagogue. My father's bridge group brought homemade dishes and trays of bagels, rugelach, smoked salmon, and deli meats. People milled around in the kitchen and family room. I looked at everyone. I kept wondering how the heck I was there with these people for Shiva for my husband. I was too young to be a widow.

In the days after the funeral, I spoke with a lot of people, but I barely recall what anyone said. My financial advisor, however, asked a question I'll never forget.

2

"Can I Keep the House?"

> "Grief does not change you. It reveals you."
> –John Green, Author, *The Fault in Our Stars*

"Are you planning to keep the house?" my financial advisor asked. The day of Scott's funeral was in mid-April. The bitter cold and dampness of March had dried out, and there was a spring warmth in the air. After the funeral, my financial advisor and I were both in my backyard talking about how I was holding up and what my plans were for returning to work. He was someone I had worked with for many years, and I trusted him. He was intimately involved with our finances and knew how much Scott and I had tucked away. When we started our careers, both of us had large law school and medical school loans to pay back. After tackling these loans, we saved as much as we could. I thought we were doing relatively well for our stage in life since we had started with nothing but debt.

When my financial advisor asked me if I planned to keep the house, I felt numb. I'd not considered moving, and I wondered why he asked me such a question. The mere thought of having to move made my empty stomach churn. Scott and I had built our home when I found out I was pregnant, and becoming pregnant had been challenging for us both. We put a lot of energy into building our home from the ground up. The builders allowed us to pick custom finishes, and we'd put thought and time into our design choices. The house was tied into my feelings about Scott, my children, and our future together. It was more than just a place where we lived. It was the cornerstone of stability in my now unstable life. Our parents had lived in their houses for decades. To me, that's what people did. Scott and I both thought our home would be our "forever house." At this point, we'd only lived in it for a little more than two years. In my mind, I had many more years to go.

"Of course, you can stay for the first year," my financial advisor added.

One of the common recommendations made to a widow or widower is to not make any drastic changes for at least one year after the passing of their spouse. In my current state, I had no intention of leaving this year or in the years to come. His question disturbed me. *Could* I keep the house? If I could keep it, could I keep it longer than just the first year? His question triggered a "looming cloud" that began to float over and follow me wherever I went. In order to make the cloud go away, I had to convince myself that the answer was that I could keep the house for as long as I wanted.

From my career in finance, I knew the best way to answer this question was to review my expenses and income. I also knew that the bigger question was not whether I could keep the house, but whether I could afford to continue living the lifestyle to which Scott and I had become accustomed. Other basic questions troubled me: Could I afford my kids' preschool, camps, child care, and college? Could we go out to dinner? Could I buy our weekly groceries? Could I afford organic produce? The emotional part of me wanted to forget these questions, run upstairs to my bed, bury my head under my warm blanket, and grieve Scott's death. The fearful part of me knew I had to get a handle on our finances to avoid severe problems down the road. I felt weirdly vulnerable—a feeling that was new and unfamiliar to me. My confidence in myself and my children's future had changed almost overnight, and I could not shake this uneasy feeling.

My financial life became more complicated between my early twenties and mid-thirties. In my early twenties, I was unmarried, lived alone, paid my own bills, and was in charge of my own banking. My financial life was simple and mostly consisted of paying bills on time and filing taxes. With large law and business school loans to pay back, I did not have a lot left over for savings, and saving for retirement was not on my radar. After Scott and I married, we bought a house and had children, so our expenses and responsibilities increased. We divided our responsibilities like many couples do. Scott handled our finances, including bills, savings, investments, and taxes. Although he consulted me, he managed it all and loved it. I was happy to have him handle the finances, because my plate was full with work, household chores and the twins.

Looking back, I question why I was not more financially involved, especially given my career. My upbringing probably contributed to my decision. In my immediate family, my father handled the finances while my mother focused on the family. These traditional male/female roles are engrained in our society, so many women take a back seat to understanding their financial picture. I learned the hard way that's a mistake.

After Scott died, I was in panic mode. I had to quickly uncover and learn our financial details to keep the house and our household functioning. All of this was now on my shoulders, and I knew our bills would not be paid unless I paid them. The seven days of Shiva came and went. One night, I entered what had once been a shared office with Scott and sat down at one end of our double-sided desk with a yellow legal pad in hand. I was a natural planner and enjoyed it. One example of this was organizing trips. Months before a trip, I would do extensive research on the best places to stay, dine and visit. I loved making lists and writing down all the things we hoped to accomplish. I carried this love of planning into the kitchen and our family activities. We had a well-organized pantry and a calendar posted on the wall containing all our kids' activities, family commitments, and obligations. The twins were involved with music classes, swim lessons, and ballet.

To get a handle on my life, I applied my planning skills to my current situation. Since Scott's death happened before the era of smartphones and before I became an avid iPhone Notes user, I wrote lists on paper pads as my way of gaining control. I began making lists of everything I could think of that had to be done to continue running our lives (things related to the house, bills, work, kids, etc.). What did I need to think about or do? What bills did I need to pay on a regular basis? How much did each monthly bill cost?

When you're going through a tragedy or crisis, a normally challenging task can seem 100 times more overwhelming. Since Scott had handled our finances and paid the bills, I had not been accustomed to tracking our family expenses. If you're in that position, it's best to take it one step at a time. Each day, I updated my legal pad and Excel spreadsheets, which contained my running tab of everything that I would need to pay for or get done. I also had a running list in my purse, which I would move to my master list as needed. Whatever I came across that day—whether I was opening a cable or electricity bill or something else—I added it to my lists. With each bill I received, I checked to make sure that my name was on it. If it wasn't, I knew I'd have to request a change. What I discovered during this process was that it was not as easy as it might seem. Some vendors were not authorized to speak with me and I had to prove that Scott had passed away in order to get my name added or keep the account open. This frustrating process took extra time and, frankly, was a real headache. Unfortunately, this can happen with more than just bills. My hope is that I can prevent you from having these same challenges.

CONSIDER THIS! *Ensure Your Name Is Listed*
- Be sure you have your name on every service account. If your name is not listed you have no authority.
- If you need to add your name, many businesses offer a change request form. If there is a valid

reason you have not added your name, then be aware what you will have to go through to access information or get something done.

QUICK TIP: *Have a Conversation about the Bills before Tragedy Strikes*

Even if you're the person in the relationship who won't be managing the bills, talk with your spouse or partner about them. Be sure to understand:
- what the bills are
- where your partner keeps a running tally
- how bills are paid (online with credit card, by check, or through auto pay)
- what passwords are used to access bills and other accounts online

These are all important things to know if you have to manage the bills unexpectedly.

Once I got my arms around what bills needed to be paid, I had to make sure I paid them on time. Missing or ignoring payment due dates could result in late fees and possibly interest. Late fees get assessed quickly and are difficult to get removed. If a bill does not get paid, it could eventually hurt your credit rating. A negative mark on your credit score can affect your ability to secure a loan, qualify for a credit card, purchase or rent a home, or something else you desire in the future. I did not want to have these consequences, so I became an expert at tracking and paying our bills.

CONSIDER THIS! *Automate Your Payments or Set Calendar Alerts on Your Phone*

- One way to reduce the chance of getting a penalty is to use automatic bill payment wherever possible. It is commonly offered by most vendors and can usually be set up online. You can choose to pay by credit card or have your checking account debited.
- If you find that having automatic payments is not working for you because you are overspending, then you can always go back to doing this manually. If that is the case, then put a calendar alert on your phone to remind you of when each bill is due and when you need to send your payment.
- Make sure to review ALL your bills, including every charge on your credit cards, to make sure you are being billed accurately. I find mistakes on a regular basis and no one is going to look out for you the way you do for yourself!

The Importance of an Accountant

In addition to leaning on my plumber and my handyman, I learned that hiring an accountant was a vital addition to my team. Most of us are familiar with regular household expenses such as a mortgage or utilities, yet a lot of people don't think about the IRS and what taxes they will owe next April. Taxes are an expense and should become part of the budget. If you're a W-2 employee—where you work for a company—your employer will usually withhold money for your taxes, so you don't have to make estimated tax payments. If you're self-employed—and you have to do your own tax reporting to the IRS—then estimated payments are an important part of ensuring you pay enough, so you don't get charged interest or penalties when you file your tax return.

Scott used to do our tax returns in TurboTax. We were both employees, had W-2s and our taxes were fairly simple. When he started his business, our tax returns became significantly more complicated. That first complicated tax preparation got dumped in my lap shortly after he passed away. Instead of reaching out to an accountant, as I should have, I tackled it myself. That was my turning point. I knew I never wanted to do my own taxes again, so I hired an accountant that I had referred clients to over the years. I still use her to this day.

While my expenses, house maintenance, and taxes were all valid concerns, my bigger challenge was the enormity of what lay ahead of me as the sole provider for my family. Worry over these things just scratched the surface of what I had to handle now. I had two-year-old twins, I'd lost my husband, I was devastated and I needed to return to my job one day soon. In some cases, people have time and space to feel their grief and process it. But in my situation, I had no down time. I felt like a pincushion being stuck all the time with life's constant demands. There was no time to grieve Scott's death. For several months, in shock, I went through the motions of living. In the middle of the night, I would wake up sometimes and cry tears of panic. Occasionally, I had a moment of feeling normal in which I almost forgot about everything, but I would soon remember and the reality of my situation would come racing back to me.

Just weeks earlier, I'd been in the grocery store with Scott. We were happy and choosing ingredients for a family dinner we would cook together. After Scott passed away, I'd shop in the grocery store and look longingly at other families living normal lives. They looked happy strolling the aisles with their children. That was once me. I thought how lucky these people were, and they didn't even know it.

I didn't think it possible that I would be happy again. I never thought I would meet anybody with whom I would have the same kind of closeness that I'd shared with Scott. Nobody I met in the future would be my kids' biological father, and that made me feel especially bad. The realization of that loss impacted me, because of the wonderful relationship I have with my dad and had with my mom before she passed. In this case, I knew that that unique blood relationship would be gone forever.

On the optimistic side, I've always felt like a survivor, so I wasn't going to give in to my circumstances. However, I did feel overwhelmed and the only way I'd gotten through such feelings before—whether it was law school or studying for the bar exam—was by rolling up my sleeves, organizing what needed to be done and doing it. My dad always encouraged me to address my challenges step by step, so that's how I approached this situation. I was going to figure out how to make this work even though I wanted to hide in my room and cry. Organizing my finances helped me feel in control.

The Importance of Having a Financial Plan and Finding Help

Logically, I knew I needed to aggregate our expenses and calculate my income to determine if I could pay our bills. But, I also knew there was more to the equation than just making a spreadsheet containing expenses and income. I knew I had to look at the big picture to make sure I was putting my family on a path for success. A couple of weeks after Scott's funeral, I returned to my job at Merrill Lynch.

One day at work, I had a meeting with my financial advisor to discuss updating my financial plan based on my new circumstances. I knew this exercise would give me the tools I needed to make more informed decisions about what I could afford and what flexibility I had to live the way I wanted to live now and in the future. I wanted organization and stability around my finances, even if the results were not what I wanted to hear. I did not want any more financial surprises.

A large percentage of people fail to have a financial plan that will help them track and achieve their goals. They might not know what a financial plan is or maybe their advisor never suggested it. If you can take away one tidbit from this book, please take away the importance of having a financial plan. Just like you plan for a trip by putting together how you will get to your destination and what your daily itinerary might look like, you need to plan for your financial future. A financial plan is the foundation of knowing your financial health. It can be analogized to getting your blood tested when you go to your internist. The results of your blood test identify potential problem areas for your health and longevity. Your doctor will continue to evaluate these markers on a regular basis to make sure your health stays on track. This is the same thing that a financial plan does for your ongoing financial health and your peace of mind.

The ingredients that go into a financial plan are things like:

- income,
- expenses,
- savings,
- tax rate,
- retirement goals,
- college funding goals,
- legacy,
- and philanthropy goals.

Your ingredients and goals will change based on your age and what stage of life you are in. Someone just starting a family will have different needs and goals than someone nearing retirement with adult children. Your plan is unique to you and will incorporate your feelings about money and risk taking. If you are living day-to-day thinking you have plenty of money to sustain your lifestyle, you may be right, or you may be in for a wake-up call when you least expect it. No matter what your stage of life, your net worth or your income level, it is **essential to have a financial plan**. It will give you confidence for today, peace of mind for the future, and a path to achieve your goals.

In preparation for my meeting with my financial advisor, I prepared an updated net worth statement (my assets and liabilities), expenses, income, and a list of what my hopes and goals were. One main hope was to keep my house longer than a year. I also made a list of what my fears were in my new role as a widowed mom of two. The outcome of this meeting gave me a reality check and some much needed guidance. I learned that we were on a steady path and that we would be okay with some spending adjustments. It also gave me a framework to use for daily decision-making about what we could afford and what we had to forgo. I was able to firmly answer the questions that had kept me up at night. After experiencing the loss of Scott and its associated challenges, I became a true believer in the benefits of financial planning.

As my career at Merrill continued, I was able to share my experience and knowledge with many of our clients, including several single women. In one case, I worked with a recent widow in her early 60s. She had never attended financial review meetings. She always found something else to do when it came to discussing money or estate planning. She was the spender in the marriage and assumed that money would always be there for her. But now, with her husband gone, she found herself like a deer in the headlights. She was worried. She'd been living a high lifestyle and loved her life the way it was. After her husband passed away, she wasn't sure if she could continue to live that way. Fortunately, in her case, her husband had done planning and purchased an insurance policy on his life. Upon his passing, the proceeds of this policy funded a trust for her benefit.

As part of her financial team, I was able to ease this widow's mind by showing her that her savings, along with her trust distributions, could cover all her expenses with proper budgeting and management. The results of her recently updated financial plan helped to establish these conclusions. It took a lot of handholding, numerous conversations, and frequent meetings, but we slowly built up her confidence. She was delighted she could still afford to do the things she loved. She and her husband had enjoyed taking their adult kids on trips. To her relief, she'd be able to keep that tradition alive and continue creating family memories.

No one wants to feel like they can't afford to go out to dinner or spend money. I experienced that concern myself right after Scott died. Often, recently divorced or widowed women stop engaging in pleasurable self-care activities like getting their hair done. I found myself doing this, too. At first, I cut out such activities, because I didn't know if I could afford them. I also felt guilty. I didn't think I deserved pleasurable experiences after Scott died.

A friend, who'd also been recently widowed, told me the honest truth.

"Michelle, go get your hair done. You really need to."

I said okay. Making that hair appointment to cover my grey patches allowed me to realize I did not have to punish myself for Scott's death. I did not deserve that, and I could afford this small luxury.

Slowly, once I got ahold of my own expenses, I began to realize that I needed to allow myself a little relaxation once in a while. These personal moments made me feel like a human being again and not a pincushion. I know that other women go through periods in which they feel they cannot afford personal luxuries. With all the demands we face today, I firmly believe wellness and self-care should be a priority and part of the budget. One of the aspects I enjoy most about my job involves helping others navigate what they can and cannot afford.

An updated or new financial plan creates confidence that you can continue your lifestyle or uncover where changes need to be made. Having this knowledge empowers us and gives us hope in the aftermath of a tragedy. By surrounding yourself with a team of trusted advisors, you will have partners to help you make educated decisions. Handling investments and finances is something that no one has to tackle alone, and organizing this key area of your life means moving forward toward a brighter future.

In my own case, once I updated my financial plan, it uncovered that I needed to reduce my current expenditures to meet my long-term goals. This was not easy to swallow, but I was thankful to have the information. Not loving the idea of cutting anything out, I prioritized my expenses into these three areas:

- **Must haves**: I need these things, or life is not fulfilling for me.
- **Want to haves**: These are things I really want, but I could live without for the time being—not forever.
- **Don't need to haves**: Things that I don't use much or don't find essential for my happiness.

You want to make these choices based on your preferences. From this list, you can determine what's most meaningful to you and where to reduce expenses. In my own case, I used to enjoy watching TV with Scott in the evening, and we had a few favorite shows. After Scott passed away, I had no time for TV or movies. I canceled my Netflix and cable subscriptions and didn't miss either one. You might have the funds to keep everything you want. Not everyone needs to cut expenses. The only way to make this determination is to have a financial plan. Each person has a unique "must have" list and should make sure they are allocating their budget to cover these essential expenses.

Not all financial planning conversations result in the need to cut expenses. I worked with one couple who realized they could retire 8-10 years earlier than they thought. They were in their late 50s with no kids and both had government jobs. They earned good salaries, and they loved to travel. They thought that they would have to work well into their late 60s in order to retire and sustain their current level of spending. We met with them several times and after completing their financial and estate plans, we showed them they could retire earlier than they'd previously thought. They were elated. Their results showed they had an extremely high probability of achieving their desired lifestyle, which included travel, time with extended family members, and hobbies. They'd never analyzed their investments and savings this way before, and they were thrilled to learn these conclusions.

They had confidence in our conclusions because we'd run the numbers in a software program that uses a Monte Carlo simulation, which provides the probability of achieving goals based on different investment returns. The results are based on data and might include such variables as assets, current age, desired college savings, income needed for retirement, and desired retirement age, amongst other things. An advisor might change input data to illustrate several different scenarios. For example, you could input your current assets, spending, and desired retirement age to calculate if you'd be able to maintain your current level of spending when you reach retirement. If there is a high probability of achieving that goal, then you might add in the purchase of a vacation home to see if you still have a high probability of achieving your cash flow needs at your desired retirement age. The beauty of having a financial plan is the ability to make updates along the way based on changing desires, needs and stages of life.

Financial Planning When You Are a Couple

I've noticed that finances and expense management can be a huge point of contention leading to disharmony in a marriage or a relationship. There is a good chance that one party or the other is not interested in participating in financial conversations. Regardless of this reality, it is important that both members of the couple try their best to attend review meetings so that they can be aware of their financial health. Even if one person has no interest in being an expert, they at least are a part of the conversation.

Financial planning can be complicated, but a good advisor will be able to present a plan in a way that allows you to understand your situation empowering you to make smart decisions. If this is not the case, then you should find another advisor or at least express your concerns to him or her.

I've worked with couples who seem to have a solid marriage and then, all of a sudden, they're getting a divorce. In one case, a wife had no clue that she was headed for a divorce. She'd never taken an interest in their finances and stopped working when her kids were born. Since having children, she'd worked part-time jobs but never had a steady income. After getting divorced, she realized she couldn't afford to do all the things she'd become accustomed to enjoying for many years during her marriage. She had to sell her house and move into an apartment, and she wasn't happy about that. It's hard living your life a certain way and then having to change it suddenly, because something out of your control happens to you. Although we cannot protect ourselves from every eventuality, we can minimize surprises by being an active participant in our finances and having a working knowledge of our own financial health whether we're single or not. I now speak confidently when I advise people that we need to take a proactive role in our finances in order to protect ourselves. In the next chapter, I share how I addressed identifying my income sources, so I could see what was possible in my new life.

3
Show Me The Money! How Am I Paying For All Of This?

"Balancing your money is the key to having enough."
–Elizabeth Warren, American Academic, Politician and U.S. Senator

An argument between my parents taught me a lesson that I live by today and that I share with my clients. My parents were married 43 years until my mother passed away at the young age of 68. While my mother had grown up selling sewing machines in her father's store, she never had a career of her own. She stayed home to raise us and enjoyed hobbies such as painting, yoga, and living a healthy lifestyle. Although my mother wasn't an extravagant spender, she liked buying jewelry and antiques. One day, I heard her yelling at my dad. She had tried to buy something, yet she wasn't able to access money on the credit card. It turned out that my dad had opened the account only in his name, and that meant she wasn't able to use it at her discretion. Although I do not recall how my father responded, I do remember that from that point forward, my mother paid closer attention to how their accounts were titled and made sure that all their accounts contained both of their names. At the end of the argument, she turned to me and said, "Michelle, make sure your name is on everything."

That was one of my early childhood memories, and my mother's words stuck with me. After Scott and I married and moved to California, we visited a bank to open new accounts and to deposit our small savings. I kept my mom's lesson in mind.

I said, "Scott, I want you to know that whenever we open a new account, we're going to title it in both of our names."

I recounted my childhood memory to him as justification for why I wanted that to happen for all of our accounts—including banking, credit cards, and the like—I didn't want to experience what my mom had gone through. Scott agreed.

Why Account Titles Matter

When I became a widow, the way our accounts were titled became extremely important and a key factor in my ability to get things done. If I was to keep the household running, I needed to be able to access money to our pay bills. I also needed to have the authority to speak with service providers. Their ability to speak with me boiled down to whether my name was on an account. If my name was not on a utility bill, for example, I had to jump through hoops to speak with a representative about an incorrect charge or service problem. I made sure to correct any oversights quickly, so I would not have problems in the future. Thankfully, most of our important accounts had my name on them because of my vigilance.

Account titling is extremely important during life, but it's also important at death. For example, let's say Susan and Phil live together but are not married. They both contribute equally to a savings account for household expenses and other purchases. Phil opened the bank account in his name and uses that money to pay their bills. If Phil suddenly passes away, Susan would be unable to access the money in the account, even though she contributed to it equally. In fact, these assets would most likely pass according to Phil's last will and testament, which may not have Susan named as a beneficiary.

If Phil does not have a will, the assets would flow by intestate succession or intestacy. This means that Phil's property will pass according to state law. Typically, state statutes name the decedent's immediate family to inherit first in varying percentages. If there's no spouse and no children, it could go to parents, then siblings, and so on. In some cases, with no closely related heirs, assets can pass to "laughing heirs." These are distant relatives who barely knew, or didn't know, the deceased. Since Susan's name was not on the account as a joint owner, she does not have legal right to these assets regardless of any verbal promises. Not all assets and accounts pass according to the terms of a will. Some assets, like life insurance, annuities, or retirement accounts, pass directly to a named beneficiary. Similarly, assets titled in the name of a trust pass according to the terms of the trust.

Along the same lines, the titling of real property, like a primary residence or vacation home, is just as important as the titling of investment accounts. Let's say Susan moved into Phil's house with the intent that they would get married one day. Several years pass, and they decide to postpone their wedding. During this time, Susan regularly contributes one half of the monthly mortgage. Her assumption is that she will be able to continue to live in the house because of her contributions even if Phil dies. She never asks to see the deed or how the property is titled. She just assumes the house will be hers, because she has been helping to pay for it all these years.

If Phil unexpectedly passes away without a will, Susan is most likely out of luck. If the deed is titled in Phil's name alone, it will pass by intestacy just like his other assets. Whether you are married or single, real property is just like an investment account. You need to make sure your name is on the deed if your intent is to have ownership of the property. You can get guidance from your financial advisor or attorney on how real estate should be titled. Depending on your net worth and estate plan, there can be different reasons for titling real property in certain ways.

The important thing is not to make assumptions that real estate will pass to you automatically just because you live there. You can find out who legally owns property by reviewing the deed. The original deed, or a copy of the deed, should be in the package of documents received at settlement. If you are unable to locate a deed, then you can obtain a copy at the courthouse. I've witnessed that a lot of women defer to their spouse or significant other when it comes to opening accounts or paying bills.

Women sometimes face rude awakenings when they become widowed or divorced. In one case, I helped a woman whose husband had run up significant debt on a credit card in her name. She had no idea the credit card was only in her name and had no idea about the charges, because she never reviewed a statement. In another case, a woman I worked with had never taken the time to review her mortgage statement. When she finally did, she found her husband had taken out a second mortgage on their house and gambled the money away. She was ultimately held responsible to pay all the money back. For your own financial security, take a closer look at the titling of all your accounts and understand why an asset is titled the way it is. If your name is not on the account or title, ask why. Was it intentional or an oversight?

CONSIDER THIS! *Proper Titling for Your Accounts*
As a couple's net worth grows, there may be reasons to title assets in a single name versus a joint name for tax planning purposes. Your financial advisor and attorney should advise you on the proper titling for your accounts. The most important thing is that you are financially secure with access to funds in the event you are left manning the ship.

Income Sources, Savings and Why They Matter

Once I got a handle on my overall household expenses, I had to figure out what income or cash flow I had coming in to cover these monthly costs. Cash flow encompasses more than just income received from a job. I use this term to include money coming in from investments, proceeds of a life insurance policy, trust income, social security income, retirement distributions or annuity payments, amongst other income sources. It's important to have a basic understanding of your income sources.

Part of understanding your cash flow includes examining your income sources and finding answers to the following questions, among others:

- What is my work salary?
- What income can life insurance proceeds provide?
- Do I qualify for any social security benefits?
- What income am I getting from my current savings?
- Do I have any income coming in from a trust created by my spouse (current or former), my parents, or grandparents where I am a named beneficiary? If so, what I am I receiving, and what is my ability to access more if needed?
- Do I receive annuity payments?
- Do I receive pension payments from my spouse's work?
- Am I at the age where my retirement savings can provide me with a source of income?

When putting together a financial plan, your advisor will look at all of the above variables and use them to forecast your ability to sustain your current lifestyle now and into the future. Just because you or your spouse have a great paying job today does not mean that you will have the same income in future years, so it's smart to plan for that potential situation.

Show Me The Money! How Am I Paying For All Of This?

Thankfully, we planned ahead, and it helped. When our kids were born, I took the advice that I give clients regarding the purchase of term life insurance. Life insurance can be used in several different ways in an estate plan. In our case, we purchased policies on each other to protect the survivor in case something happened to one of us. The best time to purchase life insurance is when you are young with few if any major medical issues. This will allow you to qualify for preferred rates with lower premiums.

Insurance provided another income source that helped my overall cash flow. Because of this planning, I didn't have to move to a smaller house or apartment. Although the insurance money was not enough for me to retire on or stop working, it gave me a cushion to preserve my sanity and stability. I was able to stay in our house, subsidize the children's activities, and maintain some semblance of our previously normal lives while adding more child care.

At that point, I wasn't spending much, because I wasn't doing a lot beyond crying and trying to survive each day. The extra income made me more secure than I would have been and allowed me to have choices. Without this cushion, I would have been extremely resentful toward Scott for leaving us. Now, the emotions I felt were mostly sadness that he was no longer able to share the wonderful family and life we'd created together. This experience illustrated for me the importance of having term life insurance.

CONSIDER THIS! *Which Type of Insurance Is Best for You?*

Term insurance:

- Used only for protection as opposed to an investment.
- Expires at the end of the term unless the policy is case premiums typically go up substantially.
- Less expensive than whole life insurance.
- All premium payments must be current for proceeds to pay out.
- The younger and healthier you are, the easier it is for you and/or a spouse to qualify along with less expensive premiums.

Other types of life insurance:

- Used for protection, estate tax planning, and as an investment, because the cash value may build up over time and can be loaned against.
- Continues for the life of the insured or until a specific age pre-determined when the policy is purchased (age 100 and sometimes even longer).
- All premium payments must be current for proceeds to pay out.

- More expensive than term life insurance because of the investment component.
- The younger and healthier you are, the easier it is for you and/or a spouse to qualify.

One of the common questions clients ask is how much term insurance to purchase. In order to know how much to buy, you have to know what your cash flow needs will be if you or your spouse passes away. Finding the answer takes conversation, number crunching, and putting your variables into a financial planning tool that can calculate your needs. The answer will be part of your financial plan.

Your cash flow needs depend on answers to the following sorts of questions:

- where you live,
- your cost of living,
- your household expenses,
- how many children you have,
- and more.

In my experience, people guess at the number—they pick numbers like $100,000 or half a million because it sounds like a lot. This is where couples really need the assistance of a professional to help them figure out an exact number that will make sense according to their lifestyle needs. They need to take college expenses and other future big ticket items into consideration. A good rule of thumb is that for every $50,000 of income you need to replace, you need $1 million of life insurance, assuming a 5% rate of return. It's better to err on the generous side, so I usually recommend more insurance coverage rather than less. The extra money doesn't hurt if you experience a tragedy, and it's not much more expensive to obtain the additional coverage.

If you're employed, you may be able to purchase life insurance as a benefit through work up to a certain cap. Although purchasing term insurance through your place of employment can be beneficial, you don't want that to be the only life insurance policy you own. Companies downsize. As good as a job might look today, it might be a different situation three years from now, and employer-sponsored life insurance is generally not portable. When you separate from an employer, you will be older and potentially have health issues that make it difficult to qualify for term insurance. I advise my clients to max out what's available through an employer, while also having an individual term policy they control themselves.

CONSIDER THIS! *Qualifying for Insurance*

In some cases it's easier to qualify for an employer-sponsored life insurance product than one you buy on your own. This is because, up to a certain amount of coverage, the insured does not have to get pre-qualified. When you purchase a policy on your own, you are required to go through a medical evaluation.

QUICK TIP: *Beneficiary Designations*
Make sure that all life insurance beneficiary designations are filled out properly and updated if a life event, such as death, birth or divorce, occurs you do not want to be surprised by a blank beneficiary designation or a designation leaving the proceeds to someone other than who you thought was named. As mentioned earlier, remember that your will does not control who is getting money from a life insurance policy. Only what is written on the beneficiary designation controls who receives it.

Social Security and Tax Benefits
Most young widows do not realize they can receive social security benefits for their minor children. This benefit can help supplement your cash flow and will continue until each child reaches the age of 18 or older, depending on your circumstances. Older widows might also qualify for social security benefits, depending on their age and the age of their deceased spouse. It is important to work with your

financial advisor and a representative from the Social Security Administration to make sure you are maximizing all government benefits available to you.

Another way to supplement your income is to reduce your tax bill. Potential tax savings vehicles may be offered by your employer. Some employers offer a FSA (flexible spending account), DC FSA (dependent care flexible spending account), or HSA (health savings account), which allow you to set aside pre-tax dollars to pay for medical or day care expenses for adult dependents or children under the age of 13. This is a good way to use pre-tax dollars for things you are already going to spend money on, and using these benefits could reduce your overall tax bill.

The HSA is for medical-related costs that accompany a high-deductible health insurance plan and can cover things like deductibles, co-pays, and other medical related expenses. The FSA and DC FSA allow you to use pre-tax dollars for things like eligible medical expenses and summer camps, day care, or after school programs. Laws can change, so be sure to ask your employer and financial professional for the latest rules and eligibility requirements for each type of plan. With the tax savings from accounts like these, it's like you're getting a coupon from the IRS!

Retirement Savings

An employer-sponsored pension plan is extremely rare to find these days, and it's naïve to think that Social Security will cover all your needs in retirement. Because of this unfortunate reality, the IRS encourages us to save for our own retirement and offers tax breaks to do so. Several different retirement plans exist—IRAs, SEPs, 401(k)s, 403(b)s, TSPs—and more. Each of these acronyms refers to a different type of plan that allows you to save for retirement while reducing your tax bill.

In many cases, I've seen that people aren't maxing out contributions to these tax-deferred vehicles, and they're missing out on "free" employer matches and tax savings. Depending on your income and employment status, there also might be other ways to tuck away pre-tax dollars.

Before you fund a retirement account, it is important to understand the specific rules that apply to the assets being placed into the account and any rule changes on the horizon. For example, retirement accounts can have age restrictions that discourage you from accessing the funds before a certain age. If funds are withdrawn prior to that age, a penalty can be assessed. In addition, retirement accounts such as IRAs have distribution requirements that mandate you begin taking distributions at a certain age or a significant penalty can be assessed. Your financial advisor should help you select the retirement vehicle right for you and educate you on the latest rules to help you maximize your savings, employer matches, and tax benefits.

QUICK TIP: *Start Saving Early*
Start as early as possible to save for retirement. The earlier you start funding a retirement account, the faster your money will grow. Retirement accounts are *tax-deferred* accounts, which means that assets can accumulate faster since you don't pay taxes on the realized growth each year. Therefore, the money in these accounts can compound at a much quicker pace than a taxable account.

Investments and Asset Allocation

With all of the household expenses piled on my plate and no spouse with whom to share the burden, I became fearful of losing money. It's quite common for women to be more risk averse than men. I felt this way, especially after losing my spouse. Although Scott had loved combing through mounds of literature comparing mutual fund performance data to select our investments, I had no desire to do that. I was too busy with the kids and my job. Instead, I began to meet with my financial advisor more often due to my change in asset level and circumstances. I trusted him and was thankful that he understood my fears and unique challenges. Due to my vulnerable feelings and risk aversion, I kept investments extremely conservative for a period of time. My advisor helped me figure out the best way to do that, so I could cover my expenses while keeping pace with inflation.

Part of the role of a financial advisor is to make sure you're properly evaluating your finances based on your new life circumstances—widowed, married or divorced. After an evaluation, you may realize that your expenses or cash needs have increased or decreased from when you were married. In addition, a widow may have a different risk tolerance than her husband did, so investment choices may need to change. Your advisor should be sensitive to **your** unique risk tolerance and comfort level with fluctuating account values based on market conditions. It is their job to discuss all options with you in a context you can understand.

If you are in a new or different life situation, it's essential to review and understand your investments and asset allocation. Part of this process might involve segregating your assets into different buckets to include an operating account and a savings account. Your operating account is the account that can be used for day-to-day expenses, and your savings account will be in place for a rainy day and future needs. Ideally, your savings would be left alone to grow and only used in an emergency or in retirement. Your advisor will help you decide how to invest the assets in all your different accounts. Each type of account will have its own purpose and investment mix, and these accounts will weave together to become the fabric of your financial plan.

During the first year after Scott passed away, my financial advisor and I met monthly just to check in and discuss how I was doing. Even if we just spent the hour chatting about life, it was helpful. Over time, as I felt more stable in my new role as a widow and single parent, I was comfortable taking on more investment risk. I am so thankful that my financial advisor did not push me, because I never would have forgiven myself if I had lost money. I was willing to forgo significant investment gains to protect my nest egg. Always realize you are in control, and do not let anyone push you into something you're not comfortable doing. At the end of the day, it's your money and you have the final say.

CONSIDER THIS! *Asset Allocation*

Asset allocation is a term used to describe an investment strategy that balances risk and reward by adjusting the percentage of each asset class in a portfolio according to your risk tolerance.

Asset allocation helps your portfolio weather ups and downs in the financial markets. Each individual should develop their own unique asset allocation based on their life circumstances:

- age,
- stage of life,
- income needs,
- desired retirement age,
- risk tolerance, etc.

A person in their 70s or 80s might have a more conservative allocation due to their need for immediate income and fear of losing principal in their non-working years. On the other hand, someone in their 40s or 50s in their prime earning years might feel more comfortable taking on risk.

Your investments and asset allocation should be treated like a blooming garden that needs to be cared for and tended to on a regular basis. As a responsible steward of your wealth, you should attend regularly scheduled performance reviews with your financial advisor. With their help, a properly diversified portfolio should allow you to withstand the financial market's ups and downs.

4
Estate Planning Basics— What If Something Happens to Me?

"Estate planning is an important and everlasting gift you can give your family. And setting up a smooth inheritance isn't as hard as you might think." –Suze Orman

Because of Scott's death, my own mortality was ever present. I didn't fear dying as much as I feared I wouldn't be around for my kids. Because of this realization and the sudden irrational fear that I could die, too, I decided to visit several doctors to make sure my health was in order. The fact that I wasn't eating or sleeping much since Scott had disappeared was not exactly what I would call healthy living. I realized I couldn't flip a switch and change my eating and sleeping habits immediately due to my grief. But, by testing for health problems, I could at least make sure that this crisis wasn't causing me to have a serious health concern. I decided to make appointments with doctors to address my major areas of concern.

I already had a sore throat, so I started with a visit to an ENT specialist. This was one of the first doctors I visited. As I sat in the examination room, my emotions overcame me. I began crying and couldn't stop. I wanted to survive to raise my kids, and I was sitting in this exam room in hopes that I could live long enough to do that. The feeling that life is ephemeral had never been something I pondered before, but I could not get that thought out of my mind since Scott's death.

I'd not visited an ENT doctor in decades. As a young child, frequent ear infections troubled me, and my mother took me to see the doctor on a regular basis. Thankfully, those ear infections cleared up as I matured. I still remembered that doctor's name and was able to locate his office. I scheduled the appointment. One of the doctor's partners was available. When the young doctor entered the room, I felt oddly vulnerable. With tears in my eyes, I told him that my husband had just passed away. By the expression on his face, I could tell he felt bad for me. At least, he got to deliver good news after examining me. My throat was fine, and I only had a cold. I had passed the first medical test of many.

Next, I visited my OB-GYN who was a family friend. He had known my mother and knew that she'd died prematurely from ovarian cancer. He understood and empathized with my concerns. I asked him what sort of test he could perform to make sure my ovaries were okay. He recommended a pelvic ultrasound as the best early detection test available. After I passed that test, I set up a mammogram appointment. Then, I met with a dermatologist and cardiologist. Thankfully, all my tests and examinations came back with good results. These appointments gave me a sense of control when I was feeling down and vulnerable. After a few months passed, I began to eat more regularly, and I vowed to exercise consistently. I'd focused on healthy living a little before, due to my upbringing, but now it seemed more important than ever. I promised myself that I'd live the healthiest lifestyle I could and teach my children to do the same. My renewed focus on health and fitness was one positive development from our tragedy.

At my urging, Scott and I completed our wills when the kids were first born. Even though the results of my doctor visits had shown I was healthy, I knew from my current situation that life can change without notice. First and foremost, I wanted to make sure that the provisions of my will and related documents would be up to date for my children. Specifically, I wanted to review the provisions that dealt with who would care for my kids in the event of my death and how my children would inherit my assets. If updates were needed, I would make them.

At Merrill Lynch, I helped many of our clients develop their estate plans from scratch or update their documents after their estate planning binders collected dust on a shelf for many years. As part of this process, I gathered information on their assets, liabilities, how their accounts were titled, beneficiary designations, and wealth transfer goals. I came across many problems waiting to happen because the legal documents didn't reflect people's desires and intentions. Life changes happen all the time. People start new jobs, divorce, and remarry. For instance, a couple married for the second time with a complicated blended family might put off updating their estate documents because they are so busy. A thorough and experienced financial advisor should make sure that all your account titles and beneficiary designations are discussed and updated on regular basis or, at a minimum, after a life event occurs.

What an estate plan involves

Warning! You know how they say you can't escape death and taxes, so we leave the story for a bit to learn about estate planning. Don't worry! The story resumes in the next chapter.

I have noticed that most people are fearful of discussing estate planning because they think it's complicated, and they don't want to address their mortality. In this section, I'm breaking an estate plan down into five pieces, so you can better understand the basics. What follows are the building blocks of an estate plan:

- Will
- Revocable living trust
- Financial durable power of attorney
- Healthcare power of attorney
- Living will

I'll go into each of these components in more detail below.

1. The Will

The first component of your estate plan is a will, which is a legal document containing your wishes for how you would like to leave your assets to your beneficiaries upon your death. For some people this can be complex and for others simple, depending upon your family situation. For example, you might leave assets outright or you might decide to create a testamentary trust (trust created upon death) within the provisions of your will to defer when your children receive their inheritance. Your will can also name one or more executors or personal representatives in charge of managing your estate until its final distribution and can contain important provisions around desired funeral arrangements and guardianship for your children.

QUICK TIP: *Three Considerations*

1. **Burial Wishes:** It is good practice to leave a letter explaining your funeral and burial desires. Although this information is included in your will, sometimes it's not accessible or read before funeral arrangements need to be made. Remember to tell your family about the letter and where they can find it.

2. **Personal Property:** Sibling squabbles that destroy family relationships can be minimized or avoided with proper communication and planning. A helpful tip is to leave a letter spelling out who gets what in great detail. For example, who gets the pearl necklace, engagement ring, specific piece of art, etc. This letter can accompany your will. Another technique is using different colored stickers. Each child is assigned a color and you affix the sticker.

3. **Digital Assets:** Make a list of your digital assets, online accounts and passwords so others can access them. Things like family pictures and videos could be lost forever without proper planning. Talk to

your attorney about these assets to make sure they are accounted for in your estate plan.

The task of choosing a guardian can be challenging. Scott and I had several conversations on this topic, and we both had siblings that were fit for the job. I highly recommend discussing the selection of a guardian when your children are young or first born. Attorneys will typically recommend naming several guardians in succession in case one or more is not able or willing to serve. The choice of guardian is not set in stone and may change over time. For example, the person you named might move to a different state or your relationship with them might change, which can cause you to want to remove them. Guardians can be updated by a simple codicil that becomes part of your will and is prepared by your attorney.

CONSIDER THIS! *Appointing Guardians*

Before you appoint a guardian, ask their permission. Not everyone wants that responsibility. The last thing you want to have happen is that you name someone, they get the responsibility, and they decline to accept their role as guardian. In that case, the backup person may become guardian or, worse, the matter gets decided in court by people who don't know you or your children.

Thinking of our demise—and who will care for our children if we pass away—is uncomfortable and even unpleasant. Please don't let that stop you from making this important decision. Your children are counting on you now—and they'll be counting on your good decisions to support them if you're no longer around.

2. The Revocable Living Trust

Revocable living trusts are frequently talked about yet commonly misunderstood. Often, people don't know that numerous types of trusts exist. Some are revocable, which means they can be changed or terminated by the creator or grantor. Others are irrevocable, which means they cannot be changed easily or without court approval. Revocable living trusts can allow for a quicker distribution of assets to beneficiaries, because the assets avoid probate if properly titled. Revocable living trusts can be a better choice for people, depending upon the state they live in, their net worth, their age, the composition of their assets and their desire for privacy. This type of trust won't reduce or eliminate state inheritance or estate taxes. A revocable living trust is accompanied by a pour-over will to capture any and all assets that are not retitled. Here are some of the benefits and drawbacks to consider:

Benefits:

- **Probate avoidance:** Revocable living trusts provide a way that clients can avoid the costs associated with probate. If your state has high probate costs, a trust could reduce the cost of settling your estate.
- **You own real estate in multiple states:** A revocable living trust can avoid the added expense of opening a probate estate in multiple jurisdictions.
- **Incapacity / disability protection:** Trusts are helpful in the event of incapacity. If a grantor who is also the trustee develops Alzheimer's, their successor trustee, potentially their spouse, would be able to quickly step into their shoes and handle financial matters.
- **Privacy:** A will becomes public knowledge when you file it during probate. Details around a trust, and how the money passes on, remain private except in some cases where litigation is involved.
- **Time:** Quicker distribution of assets to beneficiaries versus the more time-consuming probate process.

Drawbacks:

- **Increased cost:** The cost for a revocable living trust and pour-over will can be pricier than just a will. Ask your attorney if having a revocable living trust in your particular state of residence will allow your assets to be transferred more quickly to beneficiaries after you pass away. This might justify the added cost.

- **Extra Steps:** Having a revocable living trust requires attention to detail. You have to make sure that you retitle assets into the name of your trust. Your advisor can help with this, but you need to oversee the process. For example, most if not all new accounts should be opened in the name of your trust. Your attorney will give you the exact language to use when opening new accounts or purchasing real estate.
- **Tax savings:** As previously mentioned, a revocable living trust doesn't reduce state inheritance or estate taxes.

3. Durable Financial Power of Attorney

This document allows your agent, a person you choose, to handle your finances for you should you become physically or mentally unable to do so. You can choose to have this power go into effect immediately or only in the event that you are certified incapacitated by a physician. This is called a springing power of attorney. Your attorney will typically draft this document to include broad powers that give your agent or attorney-in-fact a lot of flexibility to make financial decisions on your behalf. When selecting someone for this role, consider whether they are responsible, trustworthy, and financially savvy. Most documents will name more than one agent in the event that someone is unable to serve.

QUICK TIP: *Extra Protection*
Many banks and brokerages refuse to accept powers of attorney that are not their own form documents. I recommend having both—a signed attorney-drafted power of attorney with a second supplied by your financial institution. This way you will be protected in any event.

4. Healthcare Power of Attorney

This document allows your agent to make healthcare decisions for you if you're no longer able to do so. For example, if you were unconscious in a hospital and needed medical attention, your agent would be able to make decisions regarding all aspects of your medical care. Just as with your financial power of attorney, you want to make sure your agent is up for the challenge should the need arise.

Based on the skill set of your children or other family members, you might decide to name different people to act as agents in your financial and health care power of attorney. In some cases, you can name two people to act together. However, I do not recommend that, because it can delay decisions and make it difficult to act quickly in trying times.

5. The Living Will or Advance Directive

This document outlines your wishes when it comes to being kept alive if you are in a life-threatening or vegetative state. Your living will is important, because it spells out your true intentions and can reduce confusion during emotionally trying times. Family members can disagree or feel differently about what to do, and this document takes the pressure off your loved ones while maintaining family harmony.

> **CONSIDER THIS!** *Special Considerations*
> - Because of changing tax laws and the expertise required to design a proper will, trust and other estate planning documents, I highly recommend engaging the services of an attorney versus going about this yourself or using an online form.
> - If you move to a different state, it's especially important to have an attorney licensed in that state review your will, because most states have specific and varied requirements for a will to be valid.

- If you die without a will—otherwise known as "dying intestate"—then state law will determine who inherits your assets. Who wants that?

How Often Should I Update My Estate Planning Documents?

Many people think a will is done once with no updates. That could not be farther from the truth. Your estate planning documents need to be updated every three to five years or when a major life event happens. The following is an example of why that's the case.

Sara and Sam are like most people. Shortly after they were married, over twenty years ago, they had their estate planning documents done. They have not read or touched their documents since then, and the attorney they used has retired. Their kids have graduated from college, married, and become parents. Despite the passing of more than two decades, Sara and Sam still have their original wills, which leave everything to each other. When they created them, they didn't have much money and their kids were a dream away. But now, their net worth has grown and their family structure has changed.

Family structure partly plays into Sara's fears. She worries that her spendthrift daughter, Meredith, might get

Estate Planning Basics—What if Something Happens to Me?

separated from her husband. By putting a trust in place for Meredith, Sara will be able to have the peace of mind that her daughter and grandchildren will be okay even if she's no longer around to help them financially.

Life changes indicate that it's time to review and update your documents to reflect your current situation. Sara and Sam have grown older, and their wishes have probably changed. By not reviewing and updating their estate plan, Sara and Sam run the risk that their wishes won't be followed should one or both of them become disabled or pass away. Addressing this issue can lift a huge burden off their shoulders.

You do not need to start from scratch every time you want to make a change. Wills can be updated by codicils, revocable living trusts can be updated by amendments, and powers of attorney can be amended to name different agents. Your financial advisor can talk to you about these documents and refer you to several estate planning attorneys that you can interview. It is also okay to compare prices and negotiate your fee, because attorneys can charge differently.

Since the discussions you will be having with your attorney are quite personal, it is important that you feel you can open up with him or her. You also want to feel comfortable asking questions if you do not understand something. This is your time to gain knowledge and become empowered about what happens when you or your spouse dies. Don't be bashful. Get your questions and concerns out in the open and leave your attorney's office with a satisfied feeling versus a feeling of confusion. By being an active participant during the estate planning process, you will reap the benefits should something unforeseen happen. In my own case, I was much more prepared to handle Scott's death, because I understood what my documents said.

What Is a Trust, and How Should It Be Structured?

You can liken a trust to a box with a lid on it. The lid is only opened for certain criteria, and when those criteria are met, the trustee and beneficiary can reach into the box and pull out money. In the estate planning world, we use trust provisions to restrict how much money children (or other beneficiaries) receive right away and how much gets distributed at a future date.

People's desires and opinions vary. Some only want to leave their kids a set dollar amount, even though they could afford to give them much more. Others want to give their kids as much as possible, regardless of the impact it might have on them. The question, "How much is too much?" arises often, and it's something to consider.

A well-designed estate plan, which places restrictions on when offspring inherit money, can be beneficial to your children and help keep family wealth in your bloodline in the event of divorce. Trust provisions that dole out money over time provide a child with an opportunity to learn good decision-making skills from their trustee. Some kids are spenders while others are savers. Until your child matures, it's hard to know which one they'll be, so you want to err on the safe side and use restrictions to protect them. I view these restrictions like a bed's guard rails, which keep a sleeping child safe. In a trust, the restrictions provide safety and the ability to ensure that money will be there when they need it.

I always recommend that an inheritance be distributed over a period of years. For a child under age 25 and still in school, we may only allow them to receive income from the trust with the ability to receive more, if needed, for health, education, maintenance, or support. After age 25, we might allow a child to receive a portion of the trust principal, outright, every five years until all the trust assets have been distributed.

As children become more educated about money, their spending habits can change. A spender may not always be a spender. They may learn as they go along, which is why it's important to defer when they receive the money and give them time to learn about how money works. As your beneficiary's life gets more complicated with adult responsibilities, they'll hopefully realize that it behooves them to be smart with how they use it.

With so many types of trusts and trust provisions available, I encourage my clients to speak openly about their goals and desires related to leaving money. Each family's unique dynamic will affect the selection of a particular trust type and its provisions. An attorney can help you understand what options are available and work with you to create your personalized estate plan. They will ask you questions related to your assets and how you feel about your kids inheriting money.

CONSIDER THIS! *Different Types of Trusts*

Different types of trusts exist for different purposes. An attorney can help you understand what type of trust (or trusts) makes the most sense for your family based on your net worth, the current tax laws and your thoughts on leaving money. Some trusts, known as intervivos trusts, come into existence during your life. Other trusts get defined within the provisions of your will and come to life when you pass away. These types of trusts are known as testamentary trusts.

Pros and Cons of Trusts

Pros:

- Prevent a spendthrift child from squandering their inheritance.
- Protect an inheritance from divorce.
- Shield an inheritance from litigious action. This can be a concern if beneficiaries are in a high-profile profession and subject to a lot of risk and liability.

Cons:

Trusts require

- a responsible and knowledgeable trustee,
- separate investments and accounting,
- ongoing administration and attention, and
- the filing of state and federal tax returns in the case of irrevocable trusts

An attorney can help you wade through the details to:

- determine if a trust is appropriate for you,
- consider the pros and cons of trusts, and
- mull over potential provisions.

How a Trust Can Protect Children?

Young adults are typically naïve with money. They may not value it, since they've never had to follow a budget, earn an income, or pay bills. As parents, we have to protect our children from themselves until we know they are mature enough to handle money. When a child or young adult receives an inheritance without the protection of a trust, it can ruin them. When children know they have a large inheritance coming to them, they might lose the desire to finish college or even high school. Even if they've finished school, they may lose their drive and ambition to get a job. A trust can be used to incentivize a child to get out and do something, by providing a match for any earned income they receive from working. This sort of provision can be beneficial if a child wants to enter a line of work that does not pay well, such as working for a nonprofit or teaching. The trust provision rewards a child for being productive with their lives versus looking for a high-paying job that might not fulfill them.

We want our children to be confident and functioning adults, which I consider to be someone who lives independently, holds a job, and pays for their lifestyle without financial assistance from their parents. If parents have the means to help their children financially, that's wonderful. Assistance can include helping children purchase a house, take vacations, or start a business. However, it becomes challenging for a child to become a functioning adult when their parents continue to give them handouts whenever a need arises. When a child is able to earn money through their own hard work and perseverance, they gain confidence and inner strength. These qualities help our children grow as individuals and bring them one step closer to understanding how money works and how to handle it.

In some cases, without a trust, a child might blow through their entire inheritance at a young age and not have the ability to replace those assets in the event they need them later in life. I want to be clear that there is not just one solution about how best to leave money to your children. Think about how you feel about this topic and communicate your true intentions and ideals to your estate planning team. Your estate plan can be as cookie cutter or unique as you want to make it. There is no one-size-fits-all here.

CONSIDER THIS! *Explain What You Want*

When you meet with your attorney, you can tell them what you want in everyday language. You should be open about what you want your legacy to be and your fears when it comes to your family dynamics and your children inheriting money. Your attorney will then design your documents to incorporate your unique goals and objectives for your family.

Your Choice Of Trustee

Before you finalize who will be named as your trustee, you should talk with them about the responsibility. A lot of times, I'll recommend that my clients name two different people—one as guardian and one as trustee—to provide a check and balance. This comes in handy if your named guardian is great with kids but not responsible with money. You don't want your guardian to spend trust funds on themselves instead of, or for the benefit of, your child. Your trustee should be an individual or corporation that you can rely on to be in charge of managing the day-to-day requirements of your trust.

Initially, people will often think their friend or sibling would be a good choice for a trustee. The truth is it's not a fun job. Kids may be constantly begging you for money, and you have to oversee investments and tax preparation. A lot of people don't want the hassle. In those cases, I'd recommend a corporate trustee or corporate co-trustee.

People without children may want to set up a trust for themselves or a spouse in the event of incapacity. The question becomes—without children and with an incapacitated spouse—whom do you choose as trustee? You could select an attorney, an accountant, or a corporate trustee. The answer about whom to choose depends upon your available choices and what's best for your family.

Philanthropy: Being Smart About Charitable Giving During Life and At Death

Many of us will have the desire to help a cause at some point in our lives, and we can lend support by volunteering our time and giving financially. Since you want your money to be used well for causes you care about, your advisor and attorney will review current tax laws, your adjusted gross income, philanthropic goals, and net worth to help you decide where to give and how much. Gifts can be made both during life and at death. They can create and enhance family togetherness, while leaving a lasting legacy of family values. Here are some things to think about when considering how to incorporate charitable giving into your wealth management and estate plan.

Gifts During Life:
Whether you are attending a fundraising luncheon, contemplating leaving money to your alma mater, or

selecting a cause related to an illness suffered by a family member, there is a smart way to give. Instead of taking out your checkbook and using after-tax dollars, consider using highly appreciated assets. A common example is an annual donation to a synagogue or church. Instead of paying by check, ask your financial advisor if you have any highly appreciated stock that can be used to make this donation. By gifting stock instead of after-tax dollars, you will save on capital gains taxes and, in turn, get a "discount" on your annual donation. How nice for you!

For more frequent gifts, or if contemplating future gifts, you might consider establishing an account in a donor advised fund at a community foundation, financial institution, or charity. You can name your account whatever you want and use it when making gifts to charity instead of writing a check. The year you create and fund your donor advised account is the year you receive your income tax charitable deduction even though you might not make a gift until many years in the future. It's simple to create, and you can make gifts from your fund throughout your life. You can also add to it at any time in the future and pass it to the next generation, so your children can advise on how to give the fund's assets to charity. This is a neat way to impart family values, teach your children about giving back, and work together to decide which charities to support. Some financial institutions offer donor advised fund programs with an entry level as low as $5,000.

Another strategic way to give during life is by making a qualified charitable distribution from an IRA. Because of recent tax law changes, it has become popular for people over age 70.5 to use their IRA distributions to make qualified charitable donations of up to $100,000. There is no income tax deduction for the gift, but the IRA owner can avoid including the IRA distribution as part of their adjusted gross income for tax purposes. This is a great benefit for someone who does not need the IRA income and was already planning on making a gift to charity.

CONSIDER THIS! *Regarding Matching Gifts and Tax Savings*

- **Matching Gifts**: Some corporations offer to match employee's gifts made to qualified charities. When I worked at Merrill Lynch, I would frequently make gifts to different charities and have my employer match my gift. This resulted in double the amount going to my favorite charities and was a wonderful corporate perk. Many corporations will also match employee gifts made from a donor advised fund to charity. Ask your employer if they have a matching gift program.

- **Caution:** Before making any large charitable donations, it is important to consult with your tax advisor, even after speaking with your financial advisor and attorney. Your accountant will be more familiar with your tax return and the actual tax savings you can expect to receive, if any, by making your proposed gift.

Future or Planned Gifts:

When I am reviewing a client's will and see a specific bequest to charity, I always contemplate whether there is a smarter way to make this planned gift. For example, one of the best ways to leave money to a charity is by naming the charity as a beneficiary of your IRA. They will receive the assets tax-free and your estate is eligible to receive a charitable deduction. By comparison, if you name a spouse or child as beneficiary of your IRA, then they will have to pay income taxes on distributions.

CONSIDER THIS! *Splitting IRA Accounts*

If you decide to leave part of your IRA to charity and part to your spouse, child, or other individual, then you should consider splitting your IRA into different accounts. The reason for this split is so that each beneficiary can take advantage of the maximum stretch allowed for distributions from the IRA. A charity does not have a life expectancy, and that might lead to unfavorable tax treatment for your human beneficiaries.

For larger gifts, you and your attorney might consider an irrevocable trust, such as a charitable remainder trust or charitable lead trust. Charitable remainder trusts are typically used to diversify large concentrations of highly appreciated assets. In this type of irrevocable trust, a donor gifts assets to the trust in exchange for lifetime income and an income tax deduction with the promise to give the remainder of the trust to charity upon the donor's passing. Charitable lead trusts are also irrevocable and can be used for an income tax charitable deduction. They are typically used when donors want to give annual gifts to charity with the remainder of the trust passing to kids or grandkids. Depending on the size of your desired gift, there are also charitable gift annuity programs and pooled income funds that can be used to get an income tax deduction while also receiving an income stream from a charity for your life. Lastly, it may be your desire to create a scholarship fund that continues for a number of years or goes on in perpetuity. For individuals without children or other relatives, establishing a scholarship or endowment is a powerful way to leave a legacy. The important thing to realize is that there is a smart way to give to charity.

Another thing to keep in mind is that charities are elated to get your gift, whether it comes today, tomorrow, or at some point in the future. If you made a commitment or pledge to a charity but your life has changed due to death, divorce, or some other life event, you can always ask the charity to restructure your gift or put it on hold. Do not feel ashamed or bad about this. The charity should be very empathetic to whatever you have going on in your life and be delighted to work with you so that you are financially comfortable when making your gift. One of the benefits to understanding your financial plan is that you can give with confidence and have peace of mind that you will not run out of money. Your financial team should be able to guide you on how best to make your charitable gifts given your circumstances. The lesson here is that you should pause and be strategic about your charitable legacy.

Create Your Will and Trust before It's Too Late

During my second year of law school, my parents thought it would be fun to meet in Miami Beach, Florida, for the holidays. I was excited to have a break from studying and was looking forward to relaxing in the sun. When I reached

Estate Planning Basics—What if Something Happens to Me?

Miami, I noticed my mother was not acting like herself. After a few days, she began to have extreme pain in her abdomen. My dad brought her to the hospital. After many hours and days spent in the hospital, my mother was diagnosed with ovarian cancer.

The diagnosis was a complete shock to all of us, because my mother was the picture of health. She was careful with her food choices and exercised regularly to increase her longevity. I was twenty-five when she was diagnosed, and I remember wondering how this could happen to ***my*** mother. I was scared and not ready to lose a parent. During my second and third years of law school, I flew back home to see her as often as I could. I would meet my dad at Suburban Hospital, and we would sit in her room and talk and spend time together. I felt extremely close to my dad during this time and was glad we were able to support each other. After several operations, my mother went into remission. I was able to complete my final year of study locally, so I could be with her.

The July after I graduated, I took the Maryland bar exam. In November, I received my results and was excited to share them with my mother. I ran upstairs to find her and tell her the good news.

"Mom, guess what! You now have one doctor, one dentist, and one lawyer in the family. I passed the bar exam!"

She was lying in bed. Her cancer had returned. I knew she was in pain and not feeling well, but she managed to smile when I told her the news.

She said, "Michelle, you are so lucky. You have your whole life ahead of you."

Her comment means more to me now than it did back then when I was in my mid-twenties. She'd focused on making education a priority for all three of us, and I wanted her to know that her dedication had paid off.

When I received my bar results, I was already working at a law firm as an associate. My main responsibilities at that time were drafting estate planning documents. The head attorney partnered with an accounting firm and prepared most of the estate planning documents for the firm's clients. I began my career doing legal research and drafting wills, various trusts, and corporate documents.

Little did I know that the skills learned in my first job would help my family. Due to my mother's illness, I asked my parents when they last updated their estate planning documents. It had been years. One day, after work, my boss came with me to meet my mom and dad. At this point, my mother was too sick to travel and was at home all day unless visiting a doctor. As we did together with other clients, we interviewed my mom and dad and then outlined the provisions that would go into their pour-over wills and revocable living trusts. The next day, I began to work on these documents and quickly had them signature ready. Our office notary met us at my parents' house the following day, and we went through the signing ceremony.

As I mentioned in the section where I discuss revocable living trusts, assets need to be retitled after creating and signing this type of trust. After my parents' documents were signed and notarized, I focused my time and energy on the paperwork necessary to retitle their assets. Because my parents had several bank accounts at various banks and several pieces of real estate, this was not an easy task.

The last thing I wanted to be doing during my mother's last few days was tying up loose ends with her estate plan. The night before my mother died, I sat at her dining room table and typed out deeds to retitle real estate into the name of her trust. I was doing this on my college typewriter. This took place before computers and printers were commonplace. When I finished, I walked from the dining room into the living room where she lay in her hospital bed. With her hand trembling beneath mine, I helped her sign the deeds.

I wanted so badly to ignore these necessary legal steps, but I knew how problematic the consequences could be if I did not get things buttoned up properly. This was my first lesson that waiting until a time of crisis is not the time to do your estate plan. For starters, when you are ill, you do not have a clear mind and cannot calmly think of how you want to leave your assets to your family. In addition, there is always the chance that you will not be mentally or physically well enough to sign your documents, and then no plan will be in place. I strongly encourage you to get your documents completed before tragedy strikes.

5
Mommy Guilt

"The attitude you have as a parent is what your kids will learn from more than what you tell them. They don't remember what you try to teach them. They remember what you are."
–Jim Henson

From the moment my twins were born, I felt the push and pull of parenting them while juggling the demands of my career. Although I don't have a definitive solution to the problem of mommy guilt, I have some hard-won insights. Over the years, I had put a lot of time and effort into my career. None of my success had come easily for me, yet I also knew that having our twins had not come easily either. Scott and I had issues conceiving. Since we were already edging toward our mid-30s at that point, we decided to consult a fertility specialist. After many doctor appointments, fertility procedures, and hormone injections, we learned that we were pregnant with twins.

We'd tried and failed at a previous attempt at in vitro fertilization, so the news of our pregnancy was incredible.

We were thrilled. After our failed first attempt, I thought we wouldn't be able to have children. I was devastated, but I wasn't alone. Many women experience challenges in trying to get pregnant. Our fertility declines in our late 20s and drops dramatically after age 35. For those of us who pursue higher education and prioritize our careers, this timing puts us at a disadvantage for becoming pregnant. This situation is a conundrum women must face. On the one hand, we want to be empowered and independent women, and that involves a focus on education and work. On the other hand, many of us would like to start a family. We have a finite window of time during which we can conceive, so we end up juggling a lot within a few short years—work, finding a partner, settling down, and starting a family. If we don't have kids on the earlier side of that window, then getting pregnant can become tricky.

The challenges continue. Once we have children and return to our career, many of us feel crushing mommy guilt. I don't know of a simple solution to that, but I have a suggestion. As women, we can learn from each other by sharing our experiences, and we can mentor fellow women to reduce our collective guilt. In my own case, I didn't have a sister, living mother, or older girlfriend who could provide guidance to help me reduce my mommy guilt. My own stay-at-home mother was my female role model. Her

Mommy Guilt

life priorities were to raise successful children and live a healthy lifestyle. Like many women of her generation, she started having children in her mid-20s. Because she chose not to work outside the home, she did not have the pressure of balancing a career and family. Without a mentor to reassure me that I was doing the right thing, I felt bad for not being with my kids when I was working. I was envious of other mothers who had the ability or the blessing of their spouse to be a stay-at-home mom. On top of the guilt, I felt cheated that I didn't even have the option of being with them as much as I wanted. As everyone says, they grow up fast.

I did my best to balance the children with work, yet I still felt lonely and out of place among the married stay-at-home mothers who dropped their kids off at school. Scott and I had put a lot of effort into choosing the twins' private preschool. Unfortunately, Scott never got to be part of the twins' preschool experience. He'd passed away the previous March, so I was a single mother when they started preschool at the age of two. I think I was the only single mom among the twins' classmates, and that only made me feel more alone.

Every morning, I got the kids ready for school. I could have let the au pair drive them to school, but the early morning connection with the twins was important to me. I brought them to school myself and walked them from the parking lot into their classroom. It was not always a smooth process. I remember many mornings when Chloe would decide to dress for the wrong season. On a 10-degree day, she might insist on wearing shorts and sandals. Worried about her catching a cold and freezing all day, I would force her to wear something warmer. One tip I have is to let your child wear what they want. You can manage the situation by packing other clothes in a bag to give to the teacher, or put extra clothes in their cubby. The amount of angst and energy I wasted on battling with her over outfits was not necessary.

After getting them out of their car seats, I would hold their hands as we walked into the school building. The classrooms were adorable—tiny chairs surrounded little tables. Colorful artwork covered the walls. Some days I wanted to join in the fun and stay as a volunteer, but I consistently felt the tug of work. Their preschool ended at noon. In order to keep the kids busy after school, I would sign them up for afterschool activities like cooking, ballet, or taekwondo. I knew that other mothers would pick their kids up at noon and my kids would stay late and get picked up by the au pair, and I felt guilty about that.

One spring day, I dressed in my favorite pink suit. Normally, the suit drew compliments, and the outfit made

Mommy Guilt

me feel confident. But that day, I felt self-conscious as I walked my kids into their classroom. I was the only one wearing a business suit while the other moms wore workout clothes. My suit, which I normally adored, now felt strange and out of place. Instead of feeling liked I belonged, I felt like people questioned my decision to work. I know it's possible I perceived the situation differently than it really was, but all of this felt real at the time.

Around the preschool, I felt I didn't fit in. It seemed like my fellow mothers didn't like me, and teachers felt sorry for me due to my status as a single, working mom. I felt like an outsider and never formed close friendships with the other mothers. Today, I feel strongly that we should support one another no matter what our family structure looks like or whether we work or stay home. In order for mommy guilt to change and disappear, we need to be more accepting of all unique circumstances that women face. In this way, we can support and help each other reduce or eliminate mommy guilt. Wouldn't that be wonderful!

Women and Paid Work

I struggled with my decision to work even though I enjoyed my colleagues, my profession, and my clients. My career interested and satisfied me, yet I wished that I was able to work part time or even take a few years off due to my circumstances. However, that was not an option for me at the time. Yes, I technically could have stayed home and survived for a period of years on the life insurance money. But as a financial professional, I knew how quickly money can disappear. Insurance money and savings can look like a lot at first, but it gets burned quickly with expenses. From a financial planning perspective, I determined that staying home and leaving my job wouldn't make sense in the long run for my family. If I did, I risked losing a great job and years of income and savings.

I'm not writing this book to claim there's only one right answer between choosing work, kids, or both. The decision is highly personal and the answer can be based on factors too numerous to mention here. In an ideal world, parents would be given the option and flexibility to reduce their work hours for a period of years while keeping their jobs. This would enable women to stay engaged in their career and then return to it full time as their life allows. Experienced employees are a huge asset to the workforce, and I believe it is in an employer's best interest to allow flexibility. It creates happy and dedicated employees.

What I did not fully appreciate at the time was that my inability to stay home was a blessing in disguise. As I look back, I can see how staying in the work force developed my

Mommy Guilt

skills while increasing my financial independence. In contrast, I've learned that some of the mothers I once envied did not have a similar track. Some who left their careers to become full-time stay-at-home parents felt a loss of confidence and self-worth. From my outsider perspective, the other moms had what I wanted—the ability to stay home with their kids. However, life can throw curveballs. Some of those mothers are now divorced and in a completely different financial state than when they were married. These mothers now wished they had made different choices.

Yes, hindsight is 20/20, but my message to you is that it is beneficial to stay connected to your career in some way—even if you decide to leave full-time employment. The benefits you will reap from the independence and self-worth it provides will serve you well as an empowered, independent woman. Some other things to think about if you are a woman are the unique challenges we face when it comes to saving for our own retirement. Statistics show that we typically live longer than men, leading to higher potential health and living costs, yet we have less retirement savings because of the choices we make. These choices include leaving our careers to care for young children, aging parents, or an ailing spouse. When and if we return to work, it is usually for less pay because of the time spent away from our career. Although the decision to care for loved ones is emotionally rewarding and can be personally fulfilling, it makes our road ahead to financial independence that much more challenging.

In my opinion, based on what I've seen with friends, clients, and my own personal experience, an ideal option is for women to keep their foot in the door with their career in some way, even if it's just a few hours a week. This will allow women to maintain their self-worth, their financial independence, and stay relevant. If we should find ourselves in a crisis where we need to go back to work, it will serve us well to have the relationships we have fostered from working even part time. Elsewhere in this book, I mention how a woman leaving a career should ensure her estate plan is in order to protect herself. In a worst case scenario, a breadwinner passes away and a surviving spouse is left without enough to sustain herself and her children. This can easily be prevented with the right planning.

I recognize that the decision to work or not is a personal one for every woman, and there's no right answer. Our goal should be to make our decision or accept our circumstances without the sense of guilt that we put on ourselves. I wish I could have done that earlier in my own life, and I want to help others come to that realization sooner to lessen their guilt. If you are able to find a way to stay engaged in your career when you are raising your kids, know that you will reap many benefits and don't feel guilty!

I try to find the positives in challenging situations when I can. One of the unexpected positives that I experienced from becoming a widow was the financial independence it afforded me. I cringe when I hear a girlfriend talk about hiding her shopping bags from her husband or her husband not allowing her to purchase a pair of shoes. Why would anyone want to live in submission to another? Who wants to be dependent on their spouse for permission to buy shoes? By earning and having your own money, you are more confident and independent. For starters, you can buy what you want (within reason), and your spouse will respect you more for earning your own money. The chance that resentment festers due to you spending "his" money will be reduced, and your increased confidence and independence leads to better balance in a marriage.

I want you to know that earning your own money can be worth it. Yes, it's hard. The key is finding the right balance for you, and that is what women find most challenging. Balancing family and work is tricky, and I've not seen evidence of the perfect solution to the associated struggles. If you are willing to work and stick with it, it can provide you with confidence, security, and independence. I wish I'd had a friend or mentor tell me this years ago.

Instead of feeling guilty like I did, I would have had a more positive outlook. Today, I invite you to consider that some time away from the kids is good for your own psyche and long-term wellness, and to consider that your children can happily learn and thrive from the loving influence of other adults.

Seeking the Right Child Care for Your Situation

As a single parent, it wasn't easy to manage work life, the household, and all the accompanying tasks. I felt like I was being pulled in a million different directions every day. One of the ways I was able to juggle all these different demands without a spouse was by hiring help. In a previous chapter, I talked about listing your expenses, so you can select a child care option that fits in with your lifestyle and budget. After I calculated what I could afford, I assessed how much help I would need based on my circumstances. I needed someone who could fill in for me when I had to be at the office, and I needed someone I could rely on and trust during evenings and weekends.

For me, the best option was to have someone that would be able to live in our house and be there 24-7 in case I had an emergency. My best options were a live-in nanny or an au pair. Scott and I had been through three different

Mommy Guilt

child care providers by the time the kids were two years old. Our first nanny lasted about six months and flaked out without giving us notice. Our second nanny lasted almost a year but had the habit of doing things we told her not to do, and we had to let her go. Our third child care helper was with me before and after Scott passed away, but she was not able to give me the full-time hours I ended up needing. Reliable child care is one of the biggest challenges facing working parents, and especially for those who are divorced, widowed, or otherwise single.

Whatever form of child care you choose, you can count on it being expensive. Usually, a full-time nanny is going to be more expensive than an au pair, and a full-time live-out nanny is typically more expensive than a live-in nanny. A nanny will often be older and more experienced than an au pair, yet an au pair will yield the most hours of help at the lowest cost. Although the au pair option is attractive from a cost standpoint, it comes with its own drawbacks and issues.

Scott and I had both felt strongly that we would rather have a child care provider come into our home as opposed to taking the kids to a daycare provider. Some people choose to bring their kids to daycare on their way to work. If companies provide on-site daycare, then parents may choose that convenient option. In order to feel comfortable leaving the house, you have to be confident that your children are in good hands. I had to solve the child care puzzle by weighing my different options.

QUICK TIP: *Seeking Child Care*

- When looking for a child care provider, don't be afraid to get referrals from other parents. Sometimes, that's the best way to find someone instead of hiring an agency to find one for you.
- Keep a running tab in your phone of any and all child care providers you come across from reliable listservs or by word of mouth—even if you are delighted with your helper at the time. You never know when your provider will disappear or resign, and it's good to have fallback options.

After a lot of research and mulling over options, I hired an au pair. I had read the reviews of different au pair agencies and of au pairs from different countries. It seemed that employers of au pairs from certain countries wrote good reviews, so that led me to consider an au pair from Eastern Europe. On the agency website, I especially liked one particular au pair's written bio. She sounded like she genuinely enjoyed being with kids, and the photos she posted were warm and friendly.

Mommy Guilt

Our new au pair arrived in July—four months after Scott had passed away. Outside, it was hot and muggy. The kids were in day camp during the weekdays, and I would take them to the pool in the evenings to cool off. Visiting the pool without another adult was particularly challenging. The kids loved to run in different directions on the pool deck and the swim club playground. I stuck to the baby pool, but I was still afraid one of them would drown.

Needless to say, my au pair was a welcome addition to our family. She became almost like a *de facto* spouse. We did everything together, and I treated her very well. When we would go out for lunch or dinner, I paid. I bought groceries she liked and allowed her to use the family car on her off hours. To her credit, she took on a lot of responsibility with the children, and the kids liked her. She would keep them entertained and did so with a smile on her face. Without her help, it would have been much harder for me to work and manage the household.

Our first six months together went extremely well, but things changed after a phone call on a late Friday afternoon in mid-December. When the call came, I was getting ready for our Merrill Lynch holiday party. The party was to take place at the Mandarin Oriental downtown and was usually an elaborate event. After the most challenging year of my life, things were slowly looking up, and I was even feeling at ease sometimes. However, my sense of ease and optimism disappeared when my au pair called to say she'd been in a car accident. Thankfully, the kids were not with her, and she was okay. She got in the accident on her way to pick them up from an activity. My au pair claimed the accident wasn't her fault, but the police report noted that she had been driving above the speed limit. My guess was that she was distracted by her cell phone, a common occurrence, with many young drivers.

Hiring an au pair can be a good choice in many instances; they're young and full of energy. However, this car accident highlighted one of the challenges many parents face when hiring one. Due to their young age, au pairs can lack the maturity to make good decisions. My au pair's immaturity presented itself in other instances, especially after she met her boyfriend.

After the boyfriend was in the picture, she prioritized him over her job and became less reliable. My relationship with my au pair ended when she sent me an email from her "vacation" to tell me she was pregnant and not returning to her job. She had been with us for two years at that point and was probably ready to move on with her life. That is to be expected, yet I wish she'd given me some advance notice, so I would not have been left with the stress of suddenly having no help with child care.

Mommy Guilt

Of course, these sorts of things can happen with any child care provider, but I believe there's a higher probability of this happening when you hire younger people. After this experience, I decided to hire an older full-time live-out nanny for her maturity, age, and experience. Although her salary was higher than the au pair, the investment was well worth it. She's been with us nearly nine years. In hindsight, I realize I probably should have hired a more mature provider from the start. One of my tips is to spend the extra money on the right child care provider for your situation. If you find yourself in a situation similar to mine—where you have to rely on this individual more than just a few hours a day—then investing in a person that views this job as their career is a better choice for your peace of mind and long-term sanity.

No matter what child care decision you make, you have to trust the person you hire. Consider doing a background search on the candidate to check their driving record and to look for any criminal record. I urge you to ask for referrals and actually speak verbally with them to get a sense of their work ethic and reliability. Other parents have called me as a referral source for our previous child care providers, and I am always up front and honest with them. Being a parent is hard enough, and we need to help our fellow parents when it comes to these important decisions. Child care agencies can be helpful here and will do background checks for candidates they refer to you. There are also services online that perform criminal and driving record checks. This is what we used before we hired our nanny.

A lot of us feel mommy guilt for a variety of reasons. For years, my kids would make me feel guilty that I was not at every sport event or school event. They would mention that "all the other moms" were there and ask why I had to work. My heart ached when they said that, but their opinions and comments changed over time. My children have always known me as a working mom, and they began to talk about my career differently as they got older. When they spoke proudly about my career with their friends, it made me feel good. I was surprised to hear their positive comments after so long. My hope is that I'm a role model for them, demonstrating that a woman can juggle kids and a career, especially if she gains confidence and receives support from friends, mentors, family, and work colleagues.

6

Finding Love Again—Is It Possible?

"Behind every beautiful thing, there's some kind of pain."
–Bob Dylan

Many years after Scott's passing, after I remarried, I would remember an afternoon I spilled my inner thoughts to my babysitter. The thoughts and words came fast, and my talking was more of a pep talk to myself than anything else. I spoke to her about how I deserved a complete nuclear family like the one I'd grown up in, and how I was too young to be without a partner for the rest of my life. I wanted a father for my young children, and I wanted a family structure like the one I'd had growing up.

As I spoke with the babysitter that day, I kept thinking, "I'm going to put one foot in front of the other, and I'll get through this somehow." That was my turning point toward reclaiming happiness. I knew a great life was out there, and I would have to work to for it. If you are in a similar situation, I want you to realize that you, too, have a great life out there, even if it doesn't feel like it now. An inner desire to have an amazing life can propel you forward through the days of unhappiness and uncertainty.

The family structure I grew up in influenced the type of family structure I'd desired as an adult. My siblings are nine and twelve years older, so I was the baby. My brothers attended graduate school nearby, so we lived a lot of years under the same roof despite our age differences. We shared fun and silly times. Of course, my brothers teased me as siblings do, but I felt loved. Once, my brother David took my girlfriend's keys, put them in a plastic bag, tied the bag to a weight, and threw it all in the pool. To say the least, she was not pleased. He enjoyed getting a rise out of us with these creative stunts. I fondly remember our casual dinners around the kitchen table, the ease of being with my family while we kidded around, and the trips we took to the ski slopes or to the Maryland shore. Through it all, I always knew that I could count on my family, and I wanted the same for my own children.

Even though my parents argued sometimes, they had a solid and loving relationship. I knew that they would always be there for each other. When my mother got cancer, my dad stood by her. I prioritized the qualities of devotion and trustworthiness when I looked for a partner. In Scott, I found someone with whom I could face life's challenges and thought that we'd be there for each other. I still wanted that

Finding Love Again—Is It Possible?

after I became a widow. I was so young when I lost Scott that I felt cheated of the family structure I craved. I deeply felt that I needed a partner to have that. I knew I'd never have that with Scott again, yet I was willing to accept the fact I could have it with someone else. I knew my future partnership might not be as good, but it would be good enough to fill the void.

Around the same time that I unloaded my thoughts on my sitter, I took my therapist's recommendation to join a bereavement group for young widows and widowers. The group met every Wednesday evening in Rockville, Maryland. Every week, a dozen or so people would share their experiences with grieving. Some of the members were newly widowed, and some had been coming to the group off and on for two or three years. For the first three weeks, I just sat and listened. This felt odd, because I usually contributed to most conversations.

My story felt strange, and I wasn't ready to share it yet. My husband didn't die of a heart attack or cancer like so many others. He died of suicide, and I was afraid to tell the story. How would people react? What would people think of me? My story didn't have a predictable beginning or ending, and I was self-conscious about it. When I became more comfortable with the group, I decided to open up. The room grew quiet, and all eyes were on me. After three weeks of my silence, I could tell they were eager to learn how I came to be in this group. As I shared the facts of what happened, I choked up. Tears rolled down my face. Others had tears in their eyes as they listened intently to what I'd experienced.

I appreciated how my fellow widows and widowers could relate to my pain and grief, and I eventually connected with a woman in her 40s. We lived near each other, so we'd meet up fairly often. We would share our feelings, the challenges we faced as single parents, and our desire to move forward with our lives. A few times, we visited The Palm Restaurant in Tyson's Corner, Virginia, and sat at the bar chatting over drinks. One night, she told me about a dating website she had joined.

"I signed up for Jdate, Michelle."

She explained to me that Jdate was a dating site for Jewish singles. Back then, online dating was still a new concept, so I wasn't familiar with it.

"I'm not sure that's for me," I said. I wasn't enthusiastic about it, and I felt like I had a black mark on me due to my widowhood and Scott's suicide.

Eventually, after many conversations, she persuaded me to try the dating site. She was having success, and I thought it might be a good distraction.

"Okay, I'm going to try it," I told her one day. So I signed up.

CONSIDER THIS! *Approaching Life after a Traumatic Experience*

When you decide you want a life after a traumatic experience, I invite you to go about it in the same way you'd look for a job or study for an exam. To survive after Scott passed away, I found I had to approach my life like it was a business. My business-like view might not be everyone's first-choice approach, yet it helped me navigate this traumatic and difficult time. In the case of getting my life into order, I wrote a list and then executed on it. That included seeing a therapist, reaching out to friends, eating dinner with family members at their houses, and creating a profile on Jdate. Joining the dating website became one of many tasks to accomplish, so I could try to have a happy life again.

When you're a busy person with limited time, you have to think about how you can realistically meet people. I didn't love the idea of dating again after having been happily married, but I forced myself to do it. When Scott passed away, I felt like I would be alone the rest of my life, because I was older, had two young kids, and carried the baggage of my crazy story. After I joined Jdate, I realized my fears were just fears, and that there were actually a lot of eligible men out there looking for relationships. Not only did online dating provide a distraction but it gave me hope for my future. You can fit online dating sites into your schedule no matter how busy you are with your job and kids. They're practical, and they work. You may have to go through quite a few dates, but it is a way to meet people if you're ready for it.

If you've lost a spouse, you might encounter resistance from loved ones when you express a desire to date. For whatever reason, they may not feel ready for you to move forward. I'd shifted from initially thinking I didn't deserve a happy life and feeling miserable to feeling like I wanted a good life after all. For me, reaching that new mental place took eight months. Everyone's grieving process is different, and readiness will come on its own timeline. A book I read about young widows helped me. It said not to let anybody else tell you when you're ready to meet new people or make you feel guilty for your readiness. Instead, the author said to do what feels right.

I took that advice to heart even though it was hard. My advice for other widows and widowers who are ready for dating is to put yourself out there to meet others. If your family and friends are supportive, let them know about

Finding Love Again—Is It Possible?

your readiness in case they know of someone looking for a significant other. Most importantly, don't make yourself feel guilty about your desire to seek happiness with someone else as a life partner. Remember that life is short and it is meant to be lived and lived well!

Since I needed a Jdate profile photo and did not have any recent pictures of myself, I asked my au pair to photograph me in two different outfits. The first outfit was a black strappy cocktail dress that I bought years before but never had the chance to wear. Since I had lost weight and was working out regularly, the dress looked better on me now than when I originally bought it. In my second photo, I wore a pink sleeveless top that my sister-in-law and niece gave me for my 37th birthday the previous May. When they gave this present to me, they indicated that I needed to improve my wardrobe a little. Having been in "mom mode," I'd not stayed on top of current fashions. To my surprise, I liked both photos. I was ready to take the plunge.

Once I set up my account, I'd log in after the kids were in bed and look at any messages I'd received. I still could not believe I was doing this, but it filled time on those lonely evenings. Plus, I felt good when I saw that people wanted to talk and message with me. The photos received a positive response, and that added to my confidence that I could put my life back together.

QUICK TIP: *Consider Online Dating*

When you are ready to date, I recommend online dating as a way to meet people. You can fit meeting people into your schedule no matter how busy you are. When taking your profile photo, make sure it's a good one. This photo is what immediately attracts people to you, and you want to look your best!

My first date was a setup from a family friend. Shortly after Scott passed away, this friend asked me to let her know when I was ready to meet someone. I put her off for months. On the urging of my father, I agreed to my first ever blind date. We decided to meet at Black's Restaurant, which was one of my favorite spots. With its modern and upscale décor, it attracted the young and hip. When I checked in with the hostess, she motioned me to follow her and led me to the table where my date sat. He stood up to say hello. Although I was not turned off immediately, let's just say the rest of the evening did not go well.

During this first date of my widowhood, I wondered why I was even on a date. I felt angry at Scott for putting me in a position where I had to go on a date. I'd thought I was done with dating forever. Although I loved this restaurant, I couldn't enjoy it as I normally would have. I didn't click with the date, and the meal seemed to drag. He didn't know

Finding Love Again—Is It Possible?

how to order wine—and I love good wine—and he was attacking his food with his hands while I could barely manage to eat mine. In his defense, I may have felt these negative feelings with nearly anyone. Toward the end of the date, I cried at the table. Needless to say, I didn't hear from him again.

Even after this date disaster, I pushed myself to think positively. I continued to check Jdate on a regular basis and message back and forth with other guys who showed interest. Doing this beat feeling sorry for myself. Over the next several weeks, three more guys asked me out. They seemed intriguing. After conversing back and forth, I set up dates with all three. I got ready for these dates with both high hopes and mixed feelings. On the one hand, I felt like I was in my twenties again. During these moments, I would have feelings of excitement that took me back to how I felt when I first met Scott. On the other hand, I wished I was still married again without the burden and time commitment of trying to find someone new.

I tried to be optimistic and tell myself that, at a minimum, I would meet someone new and have an evening out. Unfortunately, I developed no spark or interest with these dates despite the fact that they were attractive and kind. All three wanted a second date, and that was flattering. In the end, I wasn't interested, so I kept moving forward and connecting with others. Several more weeks passed.

On my fifth date, I met Paul. He'd messaged me via Jdate, so I visited his profile. In one photo, he wore a baseball cap and was on a rollercoaster with his kids. All of them wore huge smiles—probably screaming from fear and excitement on the ride. His profile was a little bare, but he mentioned having a career and liking it. I liked that he would be self-supporting. We sent several emails back and forth and got to know a little bit about each other before he asked me if I wanted to meet for coffee. We found out we lived close to one another when we talked about where to meet.

We decided to meet at a local Starbucks at 8:00 p.m. That night, after I put my kids to bed and checked in with my au pair, I headed out for the evening. It was the Tuesday before Thanksgiving, and I was in a good mood. I wanted to look nice—but not overdressed—so I wore jeans and a wraparound sweater. At that Starbucks, they used to have big brown comfy leather chairs near the front. Paul was sitting in one of those when I arrived. I spotted him almost immediately because he was wearing his signature baseball cap.

"Yay. He's tall and cute," I thought when I spotted him. He had a casual look—striped rugby shirt, jeans, and deck shoes—I prefer this kind of relaxed, rugged look versus an overly dressy appearance. How he looked felt right and started our date on a good note.

We introduced ourselves and got in line to order drinks. I remember keeping my drink order simple, which was different than my normally complicated Starbucks order. With drinks in hand, we sat down at a table, and I experienced immediate chemistry with him. The conversation happened easily, and I felt comfortable right away. We talked about traveling. Paul was proud to talk about his international speaking engagements, and I was eager to listen. Since I loved to travel, he was telling me about visiting South Africa and Hawaii and about his speaking topics. I was intrigued. He talked with confidence about his career, which I loved, and he was interested in what I had to say about my career.

We hopped from one topic to another with no uncomfortable lulls in the conversation. We discovered that our backgrounds were similar. We both lost our mothers in their early sixties to cancer, we were close to our fathers, and we had parents who valued a good education. We also had similar religious upbringings. Another similarity was that Paul worked and taught at Georgetown University, which is where both of my brothers attended college and graduate school. The pieces fit together nicely.

With previous dates, I'd felt like some of the guys were intimidated by my career and education, whereas Paul expressed confidence in his career and loved my background. That night gave me hope, but I felt something far bigger than hope, too. I felt that tingly feeling you get when you're excited about someone. I felt there was a chance we might work out long term, and I could hardly believe it. It seemed too good to be true!

The Starbucks was closing at 9:30 p.m. It felt like we'd only just met, gotten our drinks, and sat down when the staff began sweeping the floors and putting chairs up on tables. The minutes had flown by, because we were so consumed with our conversation and getting to know each other. We were the last customers in the coffee shop and weren't ready for the night to end.

"There's a restaurant across the street, and they have a bar that's open. Would you like to go over there?" Paul asked.

"Sure," I said. Excited to keep talking and discover more about him, I was thrilled he wanted to extend our time together.

As we ran across the street to the restaurant, Paul took my hand in his as a protective gesture. I had an immediate feeling of happiness, something that I had not felt in a long time. I was not expecting him to do that and was happily surprised. The hostess at Hunter's Inn seated us in a booth. The restaurant was dark and tired looking, but I was delighted we found a place that was open in our sleepy neighborhood. The waitress arrived to take our drink order and give us a menu. Both of us had already eaten dinner, so we decided to look at the desserts. As we reviewed our options, we discovered another commonality—a love of chocolate. We decided to share the melted, gooey chocolate brownie.

I liked the idea of sharing a dessert with Paul. Scott and I had frequently shared desserts. Sharing one with Paul felt intimate, and I thought it was a good sign we'd do this after only knowing each other a few hours. As we continued talking, we kept finding commonalities. We were both Geminis, our favorite ice cream flavor was mint chocolate chip, we both liked coffee and Indian food, and our families were originally from Russia. And we already knew we were both Jewish and lived near each other. To top it off, Paul and my brother were both orthopedic surgeons. Paul reminded me of my family, and I think that's part of what drew me to him.

At the time, I knew Paul must be curious about my widowhood, which I'd referenced on my Jdate profile, but he didn't ask me about it. I was grateful for his reserve, because I wasn't ready to talk about it during our first meeting. That night, we closed down the restaurant, and I went home smiling and feeling more hope than I had before.

We talked on the phone later that week. He was at his brother's house in Philadelphia with his kids for Thanksgiving weekend, and they were watching a movie together. From the tone of his voice, I could tell he was excited to talk with me. He suggested we make plans for Sunday, because he'd be returning home Sunday morning.

I said yes. That moment was the happiest I'd felt since meeting Paul at Starbucks.

He said, "If you're gutsy enough, why don't you come over to my house?"

"Okay, sure," I said. I eagerly looked forward to Sunday.

At the time, he was separated. When you see the word "separated" on a dating profile, it means that you should prepare yourself for drama. It means that your potential date is in the *process* of getting a divorce versus *actually* being divorced. At the time, I didn't think about the difference between "separated" and "divorced" or what either would entail in a relationship with someone. I also learned that a guy wearing a baseball cap in a dating profile photo probably has a receding hairline or is bald. At the time, I had no clue. Personally, I look for a cute face, and a nice smile.

Finding Love Again—Is It Possible?

Paul's profile stated that he wanted to meet someone who already had kids or who would be open to having more. That's what I wanted, too. We had five children between the two of us: Gillian (10), Alex (6), Daniel (8), and Alec and Chloe (both 3). And I was definitely looking for someone who wanted to be with my children. If you're over 40, it's good to open your mind to the possibility of sharing a life with someone who is divorced or has kids, especially if you already have kids yourself. People that have raised children will have a better understanding of a child's demands on your time. If you're in your 20s or 30s and you want to meet someone who's never been married, it's fine to search for that, too.

In my opinion, I don't think you should limit yourself to meeting only people who have never been married, because you might miss out on meeting your ideal significant other. When people have endured life's challenges, it adds to their character and can make them more empathetic and compassionate—and a better catch. I believe that what Paul learned from his life experiences drew me to him. In my own case, I can honestly say that I am not the same person I was before Scott's death. I am stronger and more confident in myself because of what I have been through.

Today, I'm in a different relationship than I had with Scott, but it's equally as loving and fulfilling. Originally, I thought no one would love me or my kids like Scott had. I thought I would be a widow for the rest of my life. Thankfully, I was wrong, and my life started on a new and exciting path. If you want a great life, it's out there. You have to set your mind to finding whatever makes you happy—whether that's a life partner or something else.

7

It's Complicated—
Blending Your Family with Love

"There is only one happiness in life, to love and be loved."
–George Sand, French novelist

When I next saw Paul, I felt the need to share with him how I became a widow. The subject felt like an all-consuming black cloud hanging over my head. Because I don't like to hide things and am usually open and transparent with people, I felt he needed to know this information sooner rather than later. No surprises. Subconsciously, I think I needed to know he'd still be interested in me despite my story, and I needed to know that before getting to know him better. Today, I would not feel the same way about sharing my story with a new acquaintance, yet it seemed essential to me at that time.

After leaving my driveway, it took a short five minutes to get to his house. I knocked on the door, and Paul opened it with a huge smile on his face. We hugged hello, and he offered me coffee. As we walked from his entryway through the dining room to his kitchen, I noticed he had good taste in furniture. For a bachelor, his house was nice. I was impressed. We took our cups into the family room and sat down. We both felt a combination of excitement and uncertainty. We were excited to be in each other's company, yet we felt uneasy since we didn't know each other well yet.

I sat on his worn-in brown leather sofa as his orange tabby cat, Petey, walked over to greet me. I scratched her behind the ears as Paul settled into a nearby armchair. It was cozy.

We began talking about Thanksgiving and what traditions we have with our families. I remember telling him that the holiday weekend had been special for us, because the twins celebrated their third birthday. Another bit of good news was that they were finally toilet trained, and I had bought them big boy and big girl underwear at Target. He shared in that excitement with me. I felt like he could understand it, because he had kids and knew how important it was that they were no longer in diapers.

Once we'd been talking for a while, I brought up my widowhood.

"You probably know that I'm a widow. You haven't asked so far, but I can tell you what happened."

Of course, he was curious and wanted to know. He hadn't brought it up before, because he didn't want to be rude.

I told him the story. I can't remember exactly what I told him, but I know it was detailed enough that he said, "Holy shit, Michelle, that's crazy. I'm so sorry that you've been through this."

As I told the story, I began sweating. My body trembled. I felt chills. I'd wondered if he was noticing my discomfort, but I could not control any of it. It was hard for me to tell anyone that story, because it was so horrible. I couldn't help but think the circumstances were a reflection on me. Even though I felt this way, talking to Paul made me feel more comfortable. He had a way about him that showed he cared. Just like the first night we met at Starbucks, our conversation flowed. The minutes and hours passed by like seconds.

At the end of the night he said, "I'm so glad that you told me that story, because I feel so much closer to you knowing that." He hugged me and I breathed a sigh of relief, feeling like I'd done the right thing by telling him everything.

For the many days, weeks, and months after I initially told him the story, I continued to share with him what I was going through emotionally. Paul willingly helped me process my emotions. In the beginning stages of our relationship, we'd stay up until three or four a.m. and talk about what happened and why. Through our conversations, we were trying to understand Scott's decision to commit suicide. Even though we spent countless hours talking about Scott, we never solved the mystery or completely understood it. We have come up with various theories as to why, but there's never been an "aha" moment that has revealed the definitive answer. I'll always look back on that time and thank Paul for helping me work through my emotions by talking with me about them.

On Blending Families

As our relationship developed, I was happy. I wanted Paul to meet my brothers and father to get their approval and have them share in my excitement. But, I realized I had to consider when would be the right time for him to meet Alec and Chloe. I didn't introduce him to the twins right away. He felt a similar way with his own young children. They didn't know he was dating anybody, and he didn't plan to tell them. He wanted to save that introduction until that person was set to become his long-term partner. I agreed with his approach as it was best for his kids. Since Alec and Chloe had only just turned three, I felt comfortable introducing Paul to them a few months into our relationship. They were too young to understand that they had lost their father and would not view Paul as a father replacement. Although I introduced him to the children, we held off on serious bonding until we were engaged.

We dated for nearly two years before we decided to marry. Excitement, anticipation and adventure filled our courtship. We spent as much time as we could together and traveled a fair amount. I remember a trip to Verona, Italy, as a highlight. Paul had a meeting in Verona and asked me to accompany him. I had studied in Florence during my third year of law school, and I'd always wanted to return. When he asked me if I would like to go, I immediately said yes. In Verona, we traveled to Romeo and Juliet's balcony and then took a train to Florence. I showed him the apartment I'd rented in law school in the center of town near the Duomo. We traveled well together, and this trip took our relationship to a new level. Our relationship had many high points, but we experienced challenges, too.

One challenge we would face, if we married, would involve the blending of our families. When we discussed marriage, blending our families ranked high in importance. It's easy to gloss over the complications of blending a family, but these challenges can cause big problems down the road. Realize that blending a family, especially when small kids are involved, will be hard. In fact, if young children are involved, you can count on lots of emotional turmoil ahead. This turmoil will rock the foundation of your relationship differently than in a first marriage. By knowing in advance that these challenges will present themselves in all sorts of ways, you will be better prepared to roll up your sleeves and face them head on when the time comes. Merging multiple families is an emotional roller coaster that you don't understand until you experience it. In this chapter, I share our experiences and best tips on how to handle the process.

Paul and I both came from two-parent families with no history of divorce. His first experience with divorce was his own. I was naïve about divorce and only knew about it from friends and movies. If I had it to do it over again, I would have better protected myself emotionally. I naïvely thought I could jump into a blended family, and everyone would be happy right away. I was completely wrong. I saw the situation through the lens of my own trauma, and that made me blind to the reality of what lay ahead. Even though blending families can be hard, remember that these new relationships can be a wonderful addition to your life. Relationships change over time, and it can take years for the bonds to develop in your new family structure. As challenging as it might be in the beginning, if you put in the

It's Complicated—Blending your Family with Love

time and take the high road, it will pay dividends later. I see that now in the relationships that we've developed.

When you merge families, a good therapist can help you navigate the rushing tide of emotions and educate you on the best ways to effectively communicate with your new blended family. Paul and I realized early on that we needed professional help. We so badly wanted our marriage and our new family to succeed that we were willing to do whatever it took. We asked around for names of family therapists and did our own research to find one we both liked. It took several interviews before we found "the one," so don't become discouraged if it takes a few interviews before you find the right one for you. We saw our therapist often at the start of our marriage and have continued to see him for the past 12 years. He's gotten to know our families well and has provided wise guidance—so we could deal with emotions and challenges as they arose. I consider a therapist essential for any newly blended family. It's worth the investment because the dividends will pay handsomely in the long run.

Telling Your Family about Your New Relationship

While we may think of children first when blending a family, we also have the feelings and emotions of our own parents and siblings to consider. Paul and I were excited to introduce each other to our families. We expected their reactions to be identical to ours. We'd experienced immediate chemistry and found so many commonalities and connections between our lives that we assumed our closest relatives would immediately validate our relationship. Over a holiday break, Paul asked me to drive with him to New Jersey to meet his father and brother. I was happy to go and excited to meet everyone for the first time. During this quick weekend trip, we spent time with his brother's family and had lunch with his father. I thought the weekend went well, yet Paul's family expressed concerns about my being a widow with children. Paul said his father questioned how I was working full time and raising kids successfully. I was very disappointed when he told me his father's comments, but Paul cheered me up by expressing how strongly he felt about me. He told his dad I was the person for him. Paul liked that I worked and had a career, and I liked that about him, too.

My own family questioned whether I was moving too fast into a new relationship. I'd thought my brother and Paul would hit it off right away since they are both orthopedic surgeons, but my brother had reservations. I believe that our families' comments and questions came from a good place. They wanted the best for us and for us to be sure we were taking the right next step. Although we were disappointed with their initial reactions, we were too happy to let their concerns stop us. We kept seeing each other. Months and years passed. It took a while for our families to realize our relationship was not a fleeting fancy and to settle into a new normal with us. I can happily report that our families are now close, and my brother and Paul have a great relationship.

Prioritize Your Marriage

Once you've met that special person and enter into a second marriage, I recommend putting your marriage above everything else, including kids. Our therapist recommended this, too. Your new marriage is the foundation of your new blended family, and it has to be solid. Paul and I agreed early on that we needed to have a date night at least once a week. We also agreed that we needed to take an overnight trip to a B&B or hotel every six to eight weeks. This time together has been one of the highlights of our marriage. When we go away, we might be in the midst of a disagreement or feel disconnected from each other, but we feel reconnected by trip's end. We even feel like we did when we first met. This focused time together is especially important in a second marriage, because there is so much complication swirling around you. The investment of time together will strengthen your relationship and come in handy when life's challenges present themselves.

Finances in a Second Marriage

We all bring our own baggage around finances to our relationships. How we view money develops due to our upbringing and our knowledge of finances, so everyone feels differently about the topic. In a first marriage, there's a higher probability you're younger and don't own a lot of assets yet. In such instances, couples usually combine their assets. If you're entering a second marriage, finances can be more complicated. You've likely been working for several years and may have saved for retirement. You may bring alimony, child support, savings, an inheritance, or assets from your first marriage to the new marriage. It's important to determine and list out what assets you own **before** getting married.

Before marrying, you should also know the details of your future spouse's financials. It's easy to gloss over this topic when you are in love and in the honeymoon period of a new relationship. The excitement we feel can cloud our judgment. Finding out after marriage that your spouse owes large sums of money could be devastating in more ways than one. Along those same lines, you want to know in advance if your fiancé assumes you have enough money to take care of him and his children, because it may not be possible for you to do that. Those sorts of misunderstandings can cause friction and major marital problems down the road. As difficult as it might be, you need to be willing to share your finances and expectations in detail with your partner.

CONSIDER THIS! *Discuss Expenses and Assets*

Before tying the knot, it's a good idea to have a discussion about how you will handle expenses and assets accumulated after you are married. For example, how will you pay your bills? Will you set up a joint account or will you keep accounts separate? Depending on your values, your assets and your situation, chances are you will have a better outcome when you discuss these details up front. Your financial advisor can help steer this conversation or give you questions to think about if you don't know where to begin.

In my own case, one of the things that attracted me to Paul was his stable and established career. I knew (knock on wood) that I would not have to support him, because he had the ability to earn an income. He wasn't looking to take on more financial strain. He'd paid for a divorce and was paying alimony and child support. Before Paul and I got married, we addressed the topic of our finances. Although these conversations were sometimes uncomfortable, we got through them and we are better for it today. It's also important to realize that these conversations are not a one-and-done exercise. We spent hours talking about our financial future. Try to have these conversations come from a place of caring for each other as opposed to just dollars and cents. By being empathetic, you are protecting yourself yet coming from a place of love.

One of the main reasons I wrote this book was to show you how you can have your own financial independence or, at the very least, understand your financial situation. With financial literacy, you'll enter your new relationship on better footing to blend your family with your partner's family. Of course, not everyone will have a lot of assets to bring to a second marriage. But you at least want to be knowledgeable and honest about what you have, what your new partner has, and what you expect out of your new relationship.

Prenuptial Agreements

When you are talking to your betrothed about how you will handle assets and finances, it might make sense to formalize these discussions in writing. For a second or subsequent marriage, I recommend a prenuptial agreement, commonly known as a "prenup," especially when children are involved. This agreement is created before marriage and can include provisions for division of property or assets in the case of a separation, divorce, or death. These agreements can also allow separate property to remain separate in the event the marriage ends. People find prenuptial agreements a scary or uncomfortable topic. By understanding their purpose and benefits, you can overcome your fear or discomfort.

Essentially, a prenup shows what each person brings into the marriage and then, if the marriage ends, how those assets would be divided. Another side benefit of the agreement is that it triggers a conversation about finances, which reduces your chances of being surprised by your partner's financial situation and expectations. Whether you need one depends upon your wealth, the type of assets you own, income, and whether children are a factor. I consider them essential for people with kids. In a public case, one of the Beatles didn't sign a prenup in his third marriage. He's got enough money, so he'll survive a divorce, and he made sure to protect his children with trust funds. If he becomes divorced, he won't become penniless. Unfortunately, most of us don't have his level of wealth, and we need to protect our kids and ourselves until we're further along in the marriage. Prenuptial agreements can be modified as your circumstances change. If a prenuptial agreement is signed prior to a marriage, this document should be part of the conversation during the estate planning process. If you use different attorneys for your prenup and estate plan, then be sure to give your estate planning attorney a copy of the prenuptial agreement.

Relationships Change; Your Estate Planning Documents Should, Too

In a second marriage, people often feel differently than they did in their first marriage when it comes to leaving assets to a spouse. In a second marriage, people are older and have experienced a life event that caused them to be single again. These life experiences can make people feel resentful and cautious, and they may even be less giving toward their new spouse. I want you to know these feelings can and do change over time. Second or subsequent marriages can last a long time, and people often feel an obligation to ensure their partner's financial security. I have experienced this in my own case. The cautious mindset Paul and I once shared has matured and softened as the years have gone by. Our first priority continues to be our children, but as we age together and our children mature, our estate plan will continue to evolve.

In a previous chapter, I shared a story about a widow named Marissa whose husband had set up a small marital trust for her. She was his second wife. When they initially got married, the agreement between them was that she would receive a small amount of money and the house they bought together. After many years together, his love for her had grown and his main concern was her welfare. In the event he was not there to support her financially, he wanted to ensure she could continue to live comfortably. He had the best of intentions and conveyed them to her often. She assumed everything would be okay, because she trusted him. Sadly, when he passed away, that small amount of money—and a house—is all she had to live on. Although his desire to provide for her had changed, he had not updated his documents to reflect that, even though he had the wealth to do it.

Widows are often shocked, because their husbands didn't carry out their promise to protect them financially. After a spouse passes away, the living spouse can't alter a signed document (prenups, beneficiaries designations, wills, trusts, etc.) even if their spouse verbally promised something different than what the documents state. I want to save you from that fate. To protect yourself from an unpleasant outcome, make sure the written word matches a promise that has been communicated to you.

Trusts Are Useful For Second Marriages

As previously mentioned, your estate plan will likely change—as you age, your children get older, and your net worth hopefully grows. Your children may become responsible with money when they weren't before, or they may marry someone you don't like. As a result, how you leave money to them will need to be updated in your documents. If you have young children when entering a second marriage, they need to be your first priority. In a second marriage, you want to take care of your spouse, yet you have to do so in a way that prioritizes your kids over the spouse. The spouse has the ability to earn their own money, but young children can't earn incomes and need your protection.

Typically, this is handled with a QTIP (Qualified Terminable Interest Property Trust), which is a trust placed around assets that you are leaving for your spouse. Attorneys often call these "marital trusts." They give money to the surviving spouse. However, if the surviving spouse

It's Complicated—Blending your Family with Love

gets remarried, the assets will pass on to the children from the first marriage when that surviving spouse dies. Sometimes, there's a provision that will trigger the money being cut off if that surviving spouse gets remarried. In other cases, the trust will continue to pay money to the surviving spouse, even if they remarry, but they can't drain the money in the trust unless certain provisions are met. Typically, the trustee is someone besides the surviving spouse. A trustee should balance the interest of providing the spouse with income and principal while ensuring some principal remains for the children of the first marriage.

Whenever I work with couples that want to treat stepchildren as their own, I view it as a success story. One couple that I worked with had blended their families. They both worked full time. The husband is an attorney, and the wife works in healthcare. They were both in prior marriages, and each brought three children into the new marriage. They met with me to discuss updating their estate plan to leave their joint assets equally to their six children. This couple felt the same toward each of their children whether they were a biological child or stepchild. When they first married, they didn't feel this way. Over the years, their relationships changed. This is why I counsel people not to think that the tenor of the relationships in those initial years will be set in stone. Your estate planning documents should change as your life evolves.

Adopting Your Partner's Children—Or Not?

If you're a widow or widower, the topic of adoption may arise. This will depend upon how old your kids are when you begin the new relationship and how well-formed the child-parent relationship was when the parent passed away. In my case, Alec and Chloe were only two when Scott passed away. They didn't have the chance to form a mature relationship with him. Since it was important to me to recreate the nuclear family I had growing up, I talked to Paul about my desires before we married. When I asked him about it, he replied that he'd like nothing more than to develop that relationship and adopt them one day.

We grew into the idea of adoption over time. When we felt ready for that step, I started the process. I was proud, because I prepared the adoption papers and worked with the Maryland Court System to finalize it. The process felt special to me, because we did the court proceeding with the kids. No matter what you decide, the important thing is that everybody discusses it and feels like it's the right step for the entire family. A therapist guided us through associated challenges. As you can imagine in a blended family, a father adopting his stepkids can be stressful for his biological kids. It's normal for children to feel uncomfortable, sad, or jealous with such a huge family life change. Be sure to listen to them. Our family therapist helped us all a great deal during this time.

8
Kids and Money

"So content people may not have the best of everything, but they make the best of everything. That is how you want your children to be."
–Dave Ramsey, *Smart Money, Smart Kids: Raising the Next Generation to Win with Money*

When I was growing up, our family discussions didn't involve money, investments, or how to manage finances. I wish I could have had more discussion and training around these topics, because it would have been helpful as I matured into adulthood. When I reflect on why, as a family, we did not discuss money or topics around money growing up, I think it was probably because my parents did not have these types of conversations with *their* parents.

My parents came from very little means growing up, and they were children of immigrants. They didn't receive any inheritances or handouts. My father entered the army at age 18 and remained in it for eight years. He earned the rank of captain and then left to pursue a college education followed by dental school. I don't blame my parents for my lack of financial training in childhood, but it inspired me to do the opposite for my own children.

Financial knowledge and financial literacy equals the power to navigate the world around you and make more confident and knowledgeable decisions as an adult. The sooner our children learn about money and appreciate the hard work it takes to earn it, the better off they will be. It matters so much that it pays off to start these teachings and conversations with children at a young age. I have used every opportunity possible to incorporate financial literacy lessons into daily life. Sometimes, I call these lessons, "teachable money moments." Teaching financial literacy to a child is similar to serving vegetables. At first, your child might look at vegetables in disgust, but you should smile and continue to put them on the table. Eventually, these vegetables become part of what they like to eat. It might take several meals to get to this outcome but the efforts work over time. Think about this analogy when your kids roll their eyes at you during your first teachable money moment.

My children are fortunate that most, if not all, of their needs are met and they do not want for anything material. They still become excited by the latest and greatest, but I encourage them to be savvy shoppers and research items before buying them. You, too, can encourage your kids to read online reviews, compare prices, and look for online coupons. This exercise will slow down their immediate need for gratification and teach them skills that they can use long into adulthood. We teach and use these skills now in my own family. Since my son loves basketball high-tops and gets excited when new models are released, we use that desire for shoes as a way to incorporate a lesson. Before buying a pair, we wait a few days. During this "cooling off period," he does research to find the best price, looks for deals, and reads reviews to make sure these are the high-tops he wants.

I believe that many children are given too much too easily, which leads to feelings of entitlement. This entitlement can lead to a child's expectation that they'll receive whatever they want immediately. If children are not trained along the way, they can have a rude awakening in, and after, college as they grow into adults. Being bombarded with advertising via social media and overnight shipping from online retailers exacerbates the problem and creates major challenges to raising financially sound children. With the pressures of modern day society and the need for parents to keep up with what other parents are buying for their children, it's hard to say no to our kids. Saying no requires discipline and restraint on each parent's part when children incessantly beg for something.

Children have a masterful way of making their parents feel guilty if they don't get what they want. They often complain that they are the only child in their entire school without whatever it is that they desire. A cell phone or tablet is one such object kids want. These devices cost a great deal to buy and maintain each month. In my opinion, we are setting our children up for failure if we give in to every game, subscription, or app they want to purchase unless they realize the costs associated with these devices and any related services and products. Although I reluctantly gave in to my children's request for smartphones, I stuck to my guns when it came to purchasing movies, music, apps, or subscriptions. To have "extras," they need to contribute to buying them or buy them outright.

Teachable Money Moments

As you get to know your kid's personality, you can better interpret how to explain ideas and concepts around money to him or her. You can tailor your teachings to their unique personality and what they are best capable of absorbing. I use my children's frequent requests for new things as an opportunity for a teachable financial moment. During these times, I might inform my kids that they need to allocate part of their birthday or holiday money toward a large purchase, such as a tablet or other computer device. I also hold them accountable for purchases of apps or other online subscriptions, unless they are school related. Before they had part-time jobs, this was the only pool of money that they could use for purchases, and that taught them the concept of budgeting their savings.

Allowances are useful for some families to teach financial literacy. In my own case, I found giving an allowance hard to track and maintain, so I don't do that. But I'll share two examples about giving allowances in case you want to do it. In the book, *Money Doesn't Grow on Trees: A Parent's Guide to Raising Financially Responsible Children*, author Neale S. Godfrey recommends starting to give allowances to children as young as three years of age. She recommends providing an allowance that corresponds to the child's age, so a three-year-old would receive three dollars. Her recommendations involve using a visual method—such as glass jars—to divide the allowance into three areas:

1. Saving,
2. Charity,
3. Spending.

The child can see the division of the money and observe how it grows over time. In discussing this topic with a friend, I learned that she provides an allowance only when her twelve-year-old daughter completes chores. The allowance began with the opportunity to earn up to $8.00

per week. My friend observed that her child didn't want to spend any money at all, and that meant it was impossible to teach smart decision making. In addition, the daughter wasn't motivated to do chores. My friend's solution was to increase the possible allowance to $10.00 a week while adding a rule that the child must buy birthday presents with her own money. In this way, my friend hoped to encourage at least some purchases with the child's money, so it would allow for lessons around comparing prices and making good choices.

When we shop for groceries, I'd ask Alec and Chloe to compete to see which of them could get the milk or yogurt with the newest sell-by date at the cheapest price. I ask them to check each other, and sometimes one of them finds an item at a cheaper price or with a newer sell-buy date. This teaches them to consider prices, as well as what to look for when selecting food. We love going out to eat, so restaurant dining provided another opportunity to teach the kids money lessons. We'd ask the kids to calculate the tip. They practiced math skills while learning the appropriate percentage to leave as a tip. I also showed them how taxes work on purchased items. I would ask them to add all of the prices for our food. When we received the bill, I asked them to compare their number to the number on the bill. When they saw that the bill was higher, I explained the concept of sales tax. This way, they saw that the total bill included more than just the price of the food.

Another way I have taught saving lessons was to match the amount of money that they have earned in their part-time job to help them reach their savings goal for a particular item they wanted to buy. For example, when my son was obsessed with the new Apple Watch, I said I would match his earnings, so that he could achieve his goal more quickly. This offer motivated him to put some skin in the game if he really wanted the watch. If his request was just another fleeting fancy, then he would not contribute his own hard-earned money. In our family, since the twins were about five or six years of age, I have told them they will need to have jobs someday to afford life's luxuries. They are tired of hearing it, but I hope they come to appreciate the lessons when they become adults—while they also are eating their vegetables.

In addition to the smartphone example, I have used Starbucks for teachable life lessons in budgeting. I love coffee and enjoy going to Starbucks. Coffee or a frozen coffee beverage can be made in less expensive ways, so I consider the coffee chain's products a luxury item and not a necessity. My kids love Starbucks, too. When they were younger, I got into the habit of not buying them drinks every single time we visited. By doing this, it became more of a treat or reward when they did get a beverage or something from the store. Now that they are adolescents and have part-time jobs babysitting children and teaching swimming lessons, I sometimes require that they spend their own money if they want something from Starbucks. Even though kids are earning their own money, you don't have to let them buy everything they want. Remember that you are the parent, and the answer to their request to buy something can still be no.

I think that this training will serve them well as they enter adulthood and college and need to budget and prioritize their own spending. Saying no is not easy. Any parent can attest to this. When they asked for items multiple times on each visit to Starbucks, I found myself growing tired of the requests. It would have been easier to say yes, and it took discipline on my part to say no. Sometimes, I felt bad as I watched other parents letting their kids pick out whatever they wanted. But I can see that this discipline paid off. The twins know not to expect me to buy them something every time we enter the store, and they have decided when to use their own money to purchase a treat. This same idea can be applied to any store you frequent and that you consider a luxury instead of a necessity. As parents, we teach our kids valuable budgeting lessons by teaching them to think before they buy something in these types of stores.

When the kids and I moved out of the house I had shared with Scott and into the new house Paul and I purchased after marrying, I used the experience as a way to teach the kids about mortgages. I shared with them what a mortgage was, how it works, and how someone uses a mortgage to buy a home. Although they were only five, I felt it wasn't too early to begin talking to them about these concepts. I explained that getting a loan for a house was similar to borrowing money to buy candy, because they could relate to that. By using words and concepts they could understand, I was able to begin relaying bits of useful information to them at an early age.

First, I introduced the concept of a bank as a place where money is loaned out to help people purchase things they want to buy if they don't have enough money in their pocket. I explained the concept of interest by telling them how a bank also gave people extra money to buy more candy if the bank held a person's money for them. My son, Alec, took a liking to these conversations and always wanted to hear more about these concepts and stories from my work. He enjoyed learning about money so much that we delved into conversations about buying stock in a company and what that meant. It took several life examples for the kids to grasp these concepts, but I continue to weave financially related topics into our daily lives.

When Merrill Lynch was acquired by Bank of America in September 2008, my kids were six at the time. I would talk to them about the Merrill Lynch mascot, who was a real-life bull named Dollar. At a Merrill conference I attended, Dollar was brought on stage. I had mentioned that to my children. When Merrill Lynch was acquired, I explained to them what an acquisition meant by telling the kids that Bank of America ate Dollar the Bull and that Merrill Lynch was now part of Bank of America. They still remember this conversation and talk about Dollar to this day. I am proud that my twins, at the age of 15, understand several financial concepts and continue to be inquisitive about financial matters. This is something that was not on my radar at their age, and I know the knowledge will serve them well as adults.

When to Start Discussing Financial Topics

As you can see from my examples, I began discussing finance-related topics with the children at a young age. I don't think there's a specific correct age to begin these conversations, yet I think they need to begin early. Ideally, you'll weave in teachings as relevant information presents itself. If you move, you could talk about mortgages. If you get a new job, you could talk about why you're deciding to switch careers or companies. You can always teach them the basics of banking, having a savings account, budgeting, and investing and then connect the topic to something in their life to make the subject more tangible. I recommend tying the teachable money moment into something that is happening in the child's life, so they can grasp the concept and visualize it. By doing this, there's a better chance that the child understands the concept we're teaching them. For example, a child could buy or track the stock prices of a company they know—maybe somewhere they like to eat or shop—and you can help the child monitor the value of their stock pick. It's extremely important to talk about finances with kids, and we should also encourage our children to take a finance course in high school or college. The course will give them valuable information they can use to manage their own finances, in addition to the life lessons you've taught them.

> Warren Buffet once said that the right amount to leave your children is "enough *money* so that they would feel they could do anything, but not so much that they could do nothing."

Kids and Money

As I've worked with hundreds of families with children to craft their estate plans, I have surmised that money can do wonderful things for children, but it can also be a deterrent for progressing in life. Regardless of a family's net worth, leaving a large inheritance or providing a child with everything does not do a maturing child any favors. A child who feels entitled will be less motivated to become financially independent. I strongly feel that allowing and teaching a child to become financially independent on their own, without handouts, makes them a more confident person. This will help them in other aspects of their adult life. As an example, many women remain in bad marriages, because they are financially dependent upon their husbands. They're stuck. By having the confidence that we, as women, can support ourselves, we are able to make better life choices. We're able to leave a bad marriage instead of suffering or waiting for someone to save us. We need to be able to save ourselves.

With my children, I have stressed the importance of becoming a financially independent person. As you can imagine, this concept doesn't take root overnight. Children learn through a series of discussions, events, and teachable moments as they mature into adults. The early steps might include giving a child household chores to do or by enforcing family rules established by parents. When the house rules are not followed, there are consequences. Parents should follow through with these consequences in order for a child to learn from their actions.

Early on, when Paul and I blended our families, we posted our house rules on one of the doors leading to our kitchen. Everyone in the family could easily read them there. We made the rules broad enough to encompass almost anything that would pose a safety risk to one of the kids. For example, one rule required respecting each other's personal space. If one of the kids was bothering a sibling, we would refer to the posted rule in the kitchen, hold the child accountable, and deliver a consequence. Even if the consequence we delivered was minor, it showed the kids that we meant business. They learned to respect authority. By enforcing rules, parents can teach their children they'll be held accountable for their actions—at home, school and, eventually, in the workplace.

I am sure I am like most parents in that I think my kids tune me out when I talk about financial literacy or the importance of being independent. Recently, however, my son and I were hiking in Colorado and having a deep conversation about my book and my decision to leave Merrill Lynch. On our hike, he recounted many of the financial mantras and topics I had talked to him about over the years. I was surprised. At this moment, I realized all the time and effort I had put into teaching my kids about the benefits of being independent and having an understanding of money was not a complete waste of time. They'd heard me and were listening. The concepts had sunk in. Our family values around these topics have also made a positive impact on their desire to do well in school. My daughter is motivated to do well, because she wants to be independent and have choices in life. She connects doing well in school to broadening her college and career options. She knows that she does not need to be financially dependent on her spouse to do what she wants in life. She can achieve this herself!

QUICK TIP: *Don't Try to Do It All Yourself*

Ask your financial advisor if they have any handouts or fun learning games specifically designed for children. This might help you with your efforts. In addition, as children mature and are better able to understand financial topics, it's a good idea to introduce them to your financial adviser. This will give them another opportunity to learn about money and understand the importance of working with a trusted advisor to achieve their goals.

Another way to teach kids is to let them open their own bank accounts at a young age and to review any monthly charges they have with them. I have mandated that my kids open both a checking and a savings account to hold the money that they earn in their part-time jobs. By opening these accounts, they are learning how to use a debit card and how to allocate a portion of their earnings towards spending and a portion towards savings. They are also learning the concept of interest for the money that they leave in their savings account. As their savings accounts grow, I will encourage them to diversify into different investment vehicles to increase their return. This will be a good opportunity to explain stocks, bonds, and mutual funds.

On a related note, my son has a recurring subscription to a gaming website. I make sure he knows how to review these charges every month. This is good training for when he one day has a credit card statement to review. You can never begin teaching these lessons too young. At the grocery store, I have a bet with the kids about finding a mistake in the receipt. We challenge ourselves to find an error, and sometimes we do. This helps teach them to check their receipts for overcharges. These are examples of how to engage in a teachable money moment that your child can learn from and apply later in life when they have larger sums of money to manage. If this is not a conversation you are comfortable having with your child, then ask your financial advisor for help. One of the goals of a good financial advisor is to get to know your entire family, so they have a long and lasting relationship with all generations. They should be delighted to help you.

Charitable Acts

Charitable acts can give your child perspective while stressing the importance of engaging in helping others. Children are born into their station in life. Volunteering to help those in need is one of the ways to teach your child that not everyone is as fortunate as they are. Developing perspective takes more than just telling your kids how good they have it. We need to roll up our sleeves alongside our children and create opportunities for them to gain perspective by helping those less fortunate. In our family, we have emphasized volunteering together and have done this with all five kids. We have volunteered for different organizations throughout the years, but our fondest memories include helping to provide shoes for the homeless and packing food boxes for those families that did not have the financial means to provide meals for their family.

"The Best Things in Life are Not Things" –Art Buchwald

My favorite family memories to date don't involve things. They're memories created by spending quality time with our kids on family trips. Time away from the daily distractions of work or household chores gave us the opportunity to create meaningful moments together. When the kids were young, we saved up for a special trip. After careful budgeting, we decided to take a ski trip to Snowshoe over a winter break. We'd never done something like this before. The weather was 12 degrees below zero, and the car ride was long and sinuous. As we drove up the mountain, we kept placing bets on how low the outside temperature would go. When we arrived, it was late in the evening. Without the daylight to help us navigate, we had trouble locating our hotel. Once we found it and checked in, we discovered that the rooms they had left were smaller than what we expected. Without many other options we stuffed ourselves into what was available. There were seven of us and we figured out how to make it work.

The next morning, we got up early and headed out with our ski gear on. After getting our rentals, we headed to the mountain. Earlier that morning, we had decided that all the kids would go to ski school for half a day, and then we would meet and ski together. Everyone acquiesced, and we decided where and when to meet. After lunch, we started skiing together and had a great time. It was wonderful to watch the kids wait for each other at the bottom of the hill and encourage each other when they felt scared. At the end of the day, after enjoying some hot cocoa and marshmallows, we decided to jump in the hotel's outdoor hot tub.

The kids loved it and, to this day, talk fondly about their Snowshoe trip. It's ironic to me that all I kept thinking about on the drive up was how cold it was going to be and how much complaining I would hear. I had prepared for the worst and was pleasantly surprised with the outcome. The togetherness is what made our time special. Experiencing quality time together gives children a sense that there is more to life than obtaining material things. And, as we look back on our lives, we remember time spent together more than the objects we collect. I stress this point with my children in our conversations while also creating opportunities for togetherness through family trips, get-togethers at home, and holiday parties.

Fostering Independence

When we provide children with the basic tools they need in their toolbox, they can use these tools again and again as they progress in life. As parents, we set an example by helping our children take the steps necessary to obtain their first job. For example, when my twins turned twelve, I enrolled them in CPR classes with the American Red Cross and a babysitting training course, so they'd know how to handle an emergency while they were in charge, if one arose. Later, I spoke with them about how to market their babysitting business and assisted them with advertising their services in our local community magazine. These efforts landed them on the front cover and resulted in them getting their first jobs.

They worked with me every step of the way, but I helped them with the process. By earning their own money, my children feel proud that they are capable of buying things on their own. It means more to them when they spend their hard earned money versus me buying something for them. Their jobs and their resulting incomes give them confidence that they can do for themselves now and in the future.

Preparing To Leave Money to Your Children

When I'm talking to a family about their estate plan, part of our discussion involves how to structure an inheritance for their kids. Many people don't like to think about the fact that they can pass away at any time. Even though no one likes to think about these things, it's good to plan for every eventuality. When counseling clients, I always think in terms of a worst case scenario as we review options. For instance, what if something happened to both parents tomorrow and their kids received all of their inheritance at once with no plan in place or with an outdated plan? Considerations such as these guide our conversation.

By asking questions like the ones above and below, I'm trying to create a visual in their minds of what could happen if they do nothing and pass away unexpectedly:

- What would the outcome look like for their children at their current ages?
- What would it be like for their 20-year-old to receive a large amount of money before they finished college?
- How about a newly engaged or married child, where a parent is unsure about the longevity of the marriage?

We discuss what that inheritance would look like for their kids. Most of the time, parents realize they don't want to risk the possibility of an accidental outcome, and they begin to see how detrimental it could be not to take action. They prefer to take the necessary steps to update their documents rather than gamble on how things would turn out if they did nothing. As kids mature, they'll learn how much it costs to live independently and then how much more expensive it can be when they have their own children and purchase a home. By putting a testamentary trust in place for a child, you are protecting them from themselves until they reach an age when they can be more responsible with their inheritance. When planning out inheritances, attorneys typically use age parameters for when a child should receive a chunk of money.

My own preference is to delay any major payment or distribution to a child until they are well into their 30s, so they first have a chance to mature both as a person and financially. Today, kids born in the 1980s and after are maturing later than those born in the 1970s or before when it comes to financial responsibility. They mature later in life, because many of them are putting off college or graduate school to travel or pursue other endeavors for a couple years. They are typically doing this with the financial support of their parents. They're also getting married later in life, so they won't appreciate the financial demands of raising children until later.

Instead of an outright distribution or large amount up front, I prefer to give children chunks of money in stages—this might include income payments beginning in their mid- to late-20s, and then principal distributions throughout their 30s and 40s. Along the way, they could get more if they needed it for health, education, maintenance,

Kids and Money

or support. I'm also a fan of having a child become a co-trustee of their trust once they reach a certain age. This will give them the opportunity to learn about their trust, help manage the investments in it, and work directly with a co-trustee and a financial adviser. As mentioned in Chapter 4, this step-by-step process is akin to having guard rails on your bed before you sleep in the bed by yourself.

A financial adviser or trustee can work with your child to establish a budget before they receive income from the trust and or a principal distribution from the trust. This will be helpful and start preparing the child for when they eventually receive all of their inheritance from the trust. At that point, they'll need to have a plan for how to manage the money. When they receive this large distribution, you want them to be financially savvy and mature, so that this money will be available for them if they ever have a rainy day. This trust money could supplement the income they earn from their employment. With all your efforts, not only will your kids be financially independent on their own, but they will potentially have a wonderful sprinkle of money coming to them from their trust that allows them to do anything they want to in life. That relates back to the Warren Buffet quote—and how lucky for them!

9
Eldercare—The Best Is Yet to Come

> "Grow old with me. The best is yet to be."
> –Robert Browning

When my mom passed away, my relationship with my dad grew closer. At that age, my mid-20s, I experienced a lot of changes, including becoming engaged and working full time. I frequently sought guidance from my dad and looked up to him. My father provided continual support and love for me, and I have always felt lucky to have him as my dad. Now that he is in his nineties, the love I have for him translates into my desire to make sure he is able to fully enjoy the remaining years of his life.

Up until recently, he had been able to live independently and drive his car. That changed when pneumonia put him in the hospital. My brothers and I were faced with difficult decisions about his care, including where he'd live once the hospital discharged him and he completed rehab. We knew he could no longer live without help. We considered whether he would return to his apartment with a caregiver, move to an independent retirement community, or require assisted living with round-the-clock monitoring. Part of our analysis consisted of visiting several senior living facilities and taking tours.

While working for Merrill Lynch, I often met with elderly clients at their apartments in senior living communities. Although there were a few nice homes, most of the time, I was happy to leave because the places smelled "old" and depressed me. At some of these places, it seemed like no one was truly happy in their community, including the employees that walked the halls and greeted you at the front desk. While searching for a place for my father, we experienced the vast range in quality of various senior living communities. Good ones exist, yet they need to work with your budget. To do so requires planning, which we refer to as "long-term care planning."

According to the National Care Planning Council, "long-term care planning is the process of preparing for and funding long-term care. Long-term care refers to a wide-range of medical, personal and social services for individuals who are unable to provide for their own needs for an extended period of time. This need for care from others may be caused by age, accident, illness, dementia, stroke, depression or frailty." While evaluating options with my brothers, we had to factor in that our extroverted father enjoys dining with others, playing cards, and talking with friends. If he moved back to his apartment without being able to drive to social events, he might get depressed from the lack of connection with others. With that in mind, we opted for an apartment in a retirement community that offered a lot of social activities, different restaurants, and modern amenities.

The property we chose offered the ability to step up the care to assisted living if he needed it at some point in the future. His apartment felt elegant with great lighting and modern touches. Residents and employees seemed happy and engaged in conversation, which was a welcome improvement over several other options we'd visited. Most of the residents, in their early-70s to late-90s, lived independently with or without the aid of a caregiver. Interestingly, the question my father faced was similar to the question that I faced when Scott passed away. Whereas I had to determine if I could stay in my house, we had to determine if my father could afford to live his remaining years in these new and expensive digs. Having a financial plan in place for him quickly enabled us to determine that he could afford to move to the retirement community of his choice, while also hiring a caregiver.

CONSIDER THIS! *The Cost of Long-Term Care*

We have to keep in mind that the cost of long-term care can quickly eat away at savings. When deciding on the best option for your parent, make sure you understand all the associated costs related to living in each location. For example, if your parent starts out living independently and then moves to a floor that has assisted living, what are the increased costs? Having all these details up front will allow you to plan better and make sure your parent will not run out of money in the worst case scenario. Part of going through this exercise is also to protect your finances so you are aware if you might need to kick in financially in the event that they require increased care.

The Sandwich Generation

While my father was in the hospital and later recovering in a rehabilitation facility, I had to take on responsibilities for him beyond just helping him get better and finding him a new place to live. His mail needed to be collected, his bills needed to be paid, and we had to move him from his old apartment to a new one. I wanted to help him with all these things, but I found it challenging to add these tasks to my existing stack of responsibilities as a wife, mother, and employee. In these feelings, I am not alone. According to the Pew Research Center, just over one out of every eight Americans aged 40-60 is both raising a child and caring for a parent.

I am part of the Sandwich Generation. We're defined by age—typically between the ages of 30 to 60—and by providing eldercare. In many cases, we're juggling the needs of caring for multiple family members. Imagine yourself as the inside of a sandwich with your children and aging parents as the pieces of bread. You're squished in the middle between the competing needs and priorities of family members. Grandkids, siblings, and other relatives may add additional layers. As a responsible child in the family, you may be supporting all these people. If you have a full-time career and other responsibilities, all of this can be overwhelming while causing resentment and burnout.

We have to think about how to protect ourselves when we are in the middle of the sandwich, just as we protect ourselves in the event we lose a spouse or get divorced. It behooves us to think about whether at some point in our lives we might be impacted with the needs of our aging parents. Women beware: According to a study conducted by the American Sociological Association, daughters provide the bulk of elderly caregiving. We have to think about our own family dynamics, our proximity to our parents, and which sibling would provide the most care. If you are the responsible one in the family and are a daughter, chances are this person will be you, and it helps to be prepared.

CONSIDER THIS! *Elder Financial Abuse*

When I took over paying my dad's bills, I noticed a lot of recurring charges that he had no idea he was paying. Elder financial abuse can come in many forms. We want to make sure we pick a caregiver we can trust to help our parents. We have to be vigilant when it comes to reviewing their statements and related finances. Having a trusted financial advisor can help you in this area.

My father was fortunate to have the financial means to choose the retirement community that appealed to him most. The one he liked best happened to be on the more expensive side. Other people are not as fortunate. This can happen due to a lack of planning. Most seniors acknowledge that they need to plan for long-term care needs, yet few take action. The planning gets put off until something happens that triggers this next phase of life. Without enough means to support themselves, seniors might need to rely on outside funding.

Long-Term Care Cost Concerns

When working with clients, I observed that children in charge of their parents' finances would sometimes select a lower-cost facility if the parents didn't have enough money to cover the costs of a nicer community. The children were in a difficult situation. Sometimes, they were already contributing financially but still couldn't afford to pay for the nicer place on behalf of their parents. They had to choose the less expensive option, because the extra costs were putting their own finances at risk and even causing friction in their marriage.

In many cases, the responsibility of having to financially or physically support a parent can fall on children. This can lead to resentment amongst siblings if one child pays the bills or provides care themselves, while the other children don't contribute. This inequality can even break up families and cause irreparable resentment. Your parent might feel guilty or ashamed that they have to rely on you financially. As a parent myself, I would not want to rely on my children to choose where I wanted to live. As I mentioned earlier, there is a vast difference in the look and feel of senior living communities, and some can be quite depressing. Who wants to live their final stage of life in a cold institutional setting with food that tastes like cardboard? Not me!

Eldercare—The Best is Yet to Come

How do we prevent this from happening to ourselves in our dual role as a child of an aging parent and someone who is aging ourselves? We create good outcomes by doing the proper planning now. For those of us nearing midlife and beyond, we need to think about this topic along with all the other components of a sound financial plan. Nearing my fiftieth birthday and Paul's sixtieth, we decided to buy long-term care policies. It's true that this was not my most exciting purchase, and I cannot look forward to wearing it like I would a new outfit, but it does give me peace of mind.

As I encountered the realities of eldercare with my father, I realized what a good choice it is to purchase long-term care insurance while we are still relatively young and insurable. We have our policies tucked away now, and I feel calmer about the future. I know we won't be a burden to our children. Even though I knew owning a policy was a key component to a sound financial plan, I was not able to truly appreciate the need for one until I experienced the cost of care for my father-in-law and my dad. In my father-in-law's case, we saw his savings quickly depleted as his medical needs rapidly escalated. Fortunately, he had enough to last his lifetime, but it could easily have fallen on our shoulders.

If you have a living parent or parents, you might have already experienced firsthand how expensive it can be to live to an advanced age. This is true whether you age in your own home with a caregiver or live in an independent retirement community, an assisted living facility, or a nursing home. All of these options have high associated costs that need to be factored into a financial plan. Whether it's your parents trying to determine if they can afford their new living arrangement, or it's you trying to make sure you are not going to run out of money if you live to be one hundred, the statistics show that:

- we are living longer,
- we will require long-term care at some point in our lives, and
- long-term care costs are increasing at an incredible pace.

For anyone these days, it's a challenge to afford additional care, and costs can increase dramatically in the final stages of life. Be aware that, depending upon your unique situation, it could cost significantly more than this. In some cases, people are already paying the 2047 costs for relatives with special needs.

Comparison Between Actual 2017 and Projected 2047 Monthly Costs

Home Health Care	2017	2047
Homemaker Services	$3,994	$9,694
Home Health Aid	$4,099	$9,949
Adult Day Health Care		
Adult Day Health Care	$1,517	$3,682
Assisted Living Facility		
Assisted Living Facility	$3,750	$9,102
Nursing Home Care		
Semi-Private Room	$7,148	$17,350
Private Room	$8,121	$19,712

Source: Genworth Financial, Inc. 2018

As the responsibilities from our parents fall on us, we can see firsthand the kind of burden we might be on our children if we don't plan for this phase of our lives. I learned from the experience I had when my mother was ill. I wanted to prevent a similar situation from happening with my dad, so I urged him to update his estate plan. He took my advice. This planning paid off, because we were better able to make decisions for my father when he had to move from his apartment to a retirement community.

While my dad was in rehab, his financial power of attorney empowered me to negotiate his new apartment, forward his mail, and begin to rent out his old apartment. We were able to do all these things seamlessly without the stress of an unplanned "estate planning fire drill." This lightened the burden of having to help. I was also very upfront when communicating with my brothers, so that all of us were on the same page with what I was doing and what else needed to be done. Open communication establishes trust and helps the family remain connected and harmonious during what can become a stressful time. You don't want to fracture relationships you've had your entire life over material things or your parents' care.

QUICK TIP: *Don't Try to Do It All Yourself*

If you are the most responsible child in your family, do not attempt to shoulder the entire burden yourself. Communicate with your siblings and try to delegate some of the tasks that need to be done. Be up front with what you have on your plate (remember the sandwich) and share your feelings. The goal should be to help our parents but not feel guilty about the other responsibilities we have in our lives. Ask for help so the resentment does not build amongst you and your extended family.

The good news is that we can plan for the cost of long-term care, so we are not a burden to anyone. This will help us avoid living in an undesirable place that smells institutional and has blank, white walls. I want to make sure my final phase of life is in a beautiful community that has all the amenities I have come to love. I want to be in an upbeat place with friends, good food, and lots of activities. I want to feel like the best is yet to come! One of the planning tools that helps lessen the financial burden of long-term care is a long-term care insurance policy.

With Long-Term Care Insurance:

- We can look forward to these final years instead of dreading their approach.
- We can increase the likelihood that we can afford necessary care and not be a burden to our children.
- We can select the right place for us instead of having to choose the cheaper option—or having the cheaper option selected by our children.
- We can prevent draining all of our finances and leaving our spouse or children with little to live on or inherit.

Just as we can count on death and taxes, we can count on long-term care costs increasing over time. We can also count on there being a huge need for these types of services and places with the aging of the baby boomer generation. You want to make sure that your long-term care policy covers wherever you want to live. Sometimes couples prefer to stay in their homes while a surviving spouse might be better suited to living in a community that has meals and activities on site. In my dad's case, once he was unable to drive, a community with on site activities became a better choice for him. The selection of a retirement community versus remaining at home depends on each individual's needs, but the most important part of that decision is ensuring you have the money to choose.

As a parent, one of my goals is to create harmony among my children, so they have a tight bond when they are older. I want this closeness to continue into their adulthood and eventually with their spouses and children. From working with clients and from my own experience, I have witnessed that resentment can build when an inheritance is not distributed equally between children.

CONSIDER THIS! *Don't Leave Children Wondering*

- You don't have to share your net worth or give copies of your will to your children. However, it's a good idea to let your children know who will be the executor or trustee.
- Talk with your children about how you'll leave assets to them.

Taking these steps decreases fighting among family members. To decrease the friction, spell out as much as possible for your kids and communicate it to them while you are living and coherent. We can do this ourselves as parents, and we can also encourage our own parents to do it. To prepare, we need to be able to enter a conversation about estate and financial planning with our parents. Typically, this is a hard conversation to have.

CONSIDER THIS! *How to Talk to Your Parents about Their Estate Plan*

Your parents should feel that you are more concerned about their needs versus your needs. You are having this conversation because you are looking out for their best interests. In the event that something happens, you want to protect them. Instead of asking whether they have "done their estate plan" ask pointed questions like:

- When was the last time you updated your will and trust?
- Who have you named as attorney-in-fact?
- Where do you keep your estate planning documents?
- Who is your financial advisor?

To put any of these ideas into practice, we have to engage in conversations. Due to the topics—aging and death—these can be uncomfortable, unwanted, and tricky. Please don't let that stop you. How we enter a conversation depends upon your relationship with your parents. No matter the closeness of the relationship, a parent will often look toward their children to help them as they grow older. You could take steps toward protecting your own family's finances while helping your parents by asking, "Mom and Dad, I really need for you to make sure that your estate plan is in order. If something happens to you, I want to make sure I can take the best care of you as possible." This type of request shows how you're looking to them to help you take care of them, as opposed to you wanting this information because you're nosy or want to know how much money they have.

Your parents will appreciate your consideration and respect instead of thinking you just want to see how much money you stand to inherit. The conversation should go well if you approach it from the standpoint of truly wanting what's best for your parents. If they agree, focus on helping your parents by getting the information you need and making sure their documents will help you care for them in the event of their disability. If you find this topic too difficult to broach, your own financial advisor should be able to guide you in how to talk about this subject with your parents.

In addition, it is important to note that there are attorneys who specialize in planning for elderly clients. This specialty is called "elder law." If there is a chance that your parents might not be able to financially support themselves should the need for long-term care arise, it is best to consult with an elder law specialist as soon as possible. Your parent may be eligible for government benefits, and you need to be aware of this before you shell out your savings to support them.

In the worst case scenario, the conversation doesn't go well, and your parents are not receptive. Maybe they tell you they are fine and everything is in order. If your parents are not willing to discuss the topic, at least you know that you tried and you won't look back and have regrets. Knowing in advance that the responsibility to help your parents might fall on your shoulders should motivate you to ask the questions and start a conversation. Another approach would be to give your parents some reading materials to start the conversation. If your parents live near you or even out of state, your financial advisor can provide you with estate planning attorney and elder law attorney referrals who can also help with this conversation. Good luck!

A Closing Note—Putting It All Together, Taking Action, and Empowering Ourselves

Throughout this book, I have shared my personal journey as a widow and how I found love, happiness, and financial independence. Along the way, I have covered several topics and life lessons to think about as you live your life journey. To some, my book may seem overwhelming, to others it may provide a wake-up call or possibly even validate that they are on a solid and stable path to their own financial independence.

As I think through how I want to close this book, my own uphill challenges as a woman come to mind. Many of the struggles I have faced—and will continue to face—during my lifetime are common amongst us but rarely shared and discussed. By sharing my story and bringing my challenges out in the open, I hope to draw attention to the common life events that we, as women, face along our life journey. It just so happened that my desire to write a book coincided with the Me Too Movement (#MeToo) at a time when women are speaking out more than ever before about our challenges. With the spotlight on women, it behooves

A Closing Note

all of us, no matter what age or stage of life we are in, to take action now toward ensuring our own independence. This includes not only thinking about how to make ourselves more financially secure, but also talking to our friends, daughters, and mothers about how we can help each other navigate our common life challenges.

When I was going through trying times, I often wished I had a female mentor to talk to for reassurance or even just to get a hug when I was down. I hope to be that mentor for my daughters, Chloe and Gillian. By talking to them at a young age about the need for women to be educated, have a career, participate in their finances, and start investing early, I am preparing them for a new and exciting world where women are better equipped than ever before to stand up for themselves, speak out, and control their destiny. We can all benefit from the spotlight shining on women. We are no longer a minority but a majority—with a voice.

I never thought I would find happiness again after my first husband passed away. I thought my life was over, and I thought no one would love me the way he had. I was wrong. If you are reading this book and feel the same way, please remember that an amazing life is out there waiting for you. Stand up, take action, and empower yourself—the best is yet to come!

Appendix

In this book, I have highlighted why it is important to be your own advocate when it comes to your finances and estate plan. I have also given you case studies and examples that illustrate what can happen if you choose to ignore these topics. To help you on your path toward financial literacy, I have put together some questions and checklists. I have also included tips to consider when searching for a good financial advisor, as well as things to think about when looking for an estate planning attorney. Remember that not every advisor or attorney is going to be a good fit for you. By reading my tips and search pointers, you will be better prepared to make decisions on who to include as part of your financial team and what to tackle next on your financial to do list.

I. Estate Planning Stress Test: How Prepared Are You?

Having a well thought out estate plan is one of the most important things you can do for your family. Understanding what your estate plan says is one of the most important things you can do for your own peace of mind and financial security. The following 20 questions are

Appendix

designed to help you assess your current state of affairs and what sort of updates or additional planning you might need to put in place.

Remember that estate planning is an ongoing process. Your documents need to be reviewed and possibly updated after a life transition, a significant change in net worth, or a change in tax laws. Once in place, your attorney and financial advisor should help you navigate this process on a continual basis to make sure you are on track to meet your personal and legacy goals.

1. Do you and your spouse/partner have a will or revocable living trust?
2. Have you reviewed your will and trust within the last 3 to 5 years?
3. Have you had any major life events occur in your family—such as a death, divorce, adoption, or birth—since you executed your estate planning documents?
4. Have there been any changes in federal or state tax laws since you updated your will and trust last?
5. Has your net worth significantly changed since you last updated your estate planning documents?
6. If your net worth has increased, have you updated the provisions of any testamentary trusts you have

in place for your children so they do not blow through their inheritance?
7. Have you named a guardian for your minor children? Have you discussed this appointment with them to make sure they want the job?
8. Are the guardians you have named still appropriate choices for your kids?
9. Have you named an executor and/or trustee? Will they have the time and knowledge to fulfill their responsibilities?
10. Have you considered the family dynamics that could occur by naming one child as an executor and/or trustee over your other children?
11. Do you have a financial power of attorney in place so that your attorney-in-fact can help you make financial decisions in the event you are unable to do so or incapacitated?
12. Do you have a health care power of attorney and living will in place to make sure that your wishes are carried out if you are unable to make health care decisions for yourself?
13. Have you titled all of your assets appropriately? If you have a revocable living trust, have you titled your assets in the name of the trust?

Appendix

14. Have you reviewed the beneficiary designations on all your retirement accounts, life insurance, and annuity contracts? Do these beneficiary designations compliment the provisions of your will and/or trust?
15. If you are in a second marriage or blended family, have you made sure that your estate plan addresses your desires around providing for your current spouse, as well as children from a prior marriage?
16. Do you have the appropriate life insurance in place to provide for your family?
17. If you have a family member with a disability or special needs, have you created a special needs trust to provide for them while protecting any disability benefits they receive?
18. If you are leaving assets to charity, have you done this in the most tax efficient and beneficial way possible?
19. If you are caring for aging parents, have you talked to them about whether their estate planning documents are up to date? Do you know where the originals are located and the names of their advisors?
20. Does your executor and/or trustee know where your original estate planning documents are

located and the contact information for your attorney and advisor?

II. Finding an Estate Planning Attorney That's Right for You

When I have a health concern, one of the first things I think about is what type of doctor I should go see. Although I have an internist, I prefer to use specialists for health issues that crop up from time to time. For example, if my back hurts, I would look for an orthopedist who is a spine specialist. The same holds true for finding a lawyer to design or update your estate plan. You need to find one that has years of training in this area and not one who does estate planning as part of their general practice. The reason is that tax laws are complicated and constantly changing. The effectiveness of an estate plan depends on your lawyer's knowledge of current law and how well they draft estate planning documents.

I have had clients bring in beautiful leather binders with wills that were over 100 pages long, but the documents were not carefully drafted. When choosing an attorney, you want to make sure they are drafting documents unique to your needs and circumstances, versus using standard provisions that are part of a "how to do estate planning seminar" they

Appendix

attended to broaden their law practice. Here are 10 tips that will help you find a qualified estate planning attorney:

1. Ask your financial advisor or CPA: Your advisor and CPA work with estate planning attorneys on a regular basis and probably have their favorite ones that roll off the tip of their tongue. You can also ask them who did their own estate planning documents.

2. Make sure the attorney you choose has plenty of clients with your size estate. Depending on the complexity of your assets and your net worth, you might need an attorney that specializes in higher net worth clients.

3. Make sure your attorney has a specialty in trust and estate law. You can ask your local bar association, as well as review their resume. Look for an attorney who writes books or whitepapers, or who speaks about estate planning to groups.

4. Ask other attorneys you have worked with in the community who they would recommend.

5. Get a few names and interview them by phone and/or face-to-face. You want to make sure you connect with this individual. Estate planning is very personal, and you want to feel at ease and comfortable talking to them. If they communicate

in legalese or like a robot, chances are you will not understand what your documents say, and this is not the result we want.

6. Don't be afraid to ask how much your attorney is going to charge for new documents or updates to existing documents. Attorneys can bill differently. Some bill by the hour, and some have a fixed fee for a package of basic documents. Remember that fees are negotiable, so don't be afraid to advocate for yourself just like you would with any other vendor.

7. Ask how long the process will take, and hold your attorney to this timeline. I have seen documents take years to be signed and, in some cases, they never get signed and people pass away. A best practice is to set a time deadline in your mind like before you leave for a vacation or before the holidays start. People come up with every excuse in the book for putting off signing their documents. In the back of your mind, remember that you are doing this for your family and to protect yourself…it's in your best interest to get this done!

8. Take good notes so that you remember your homework and things that need to be done to prepare for your initial or follow-up meetings. I

Appendix

usually do this in my smart phone so that I have these notes with me at all times.

9. Read the summary memo that usually accompanies your estate planning documents. This memo typically gives you instructions on how to title your assets and how to fill out beneficiary designations. Many people unfortunately ignore these instructions and this is where problems occur.

10. Store your documents in a fire-proof and water-proof safe or in a file cabinet in your home office. Communicate where your documents are located (and the combination to access them) to your spouse, significant other, or your executor/trustee. Many people store their original documents in a bank safety deposit box. I advise against this, because it might be more trouble than it's worth to access them when the need arises. In most cases, banks require a court order to allow someone not listed on the account to gain access. Other people store their originals with their attorney. This is acceptable, but I prefer to hold onto them myself in case the attorney changes firms, I decide to switch attorneys, or I move out of the area. The final decision is up to you.

III. The Value of Having a Financial Advisor and How to Find a Good One

Since the internet has endless information about investing, should you still work with a financial advisor? The answer is a resounding YES. As you have seen from my personal journey, having a financial advisor was a huge benefit for me and gave me the financial knowledge I needed during an extremely difficult time in my life. Working with a financial advisor is not just about learning the latest stock tip or finding the best performing mutual fund. Working with a financial advisor is about laying the foundation of your financial wellness and creating your own personal road map to achieve your life's goals.

Just like finding an estate planning attorney takes thought and effort, finding a good financial advisor requires some effort on your part. Remember that you will be in contact with this person regularly and throughout your life. During my years at Merrill Lynch, I learned that not all financial advisors are created equal. You want to find one that is a good match for you and one that has the experience to guide you properly.

Here are 15 tips and insights to help you:

1. Referral from a trusted friend – this can be a good place to start, but it's important to do your own due diligence to make sure the advisor checks out.

Appendix

2. Check references – ask the advisor for 2 or 3 references and actually speak with them. Have your list of questions handy.
3. Consider years of experience. A little gray hair is good when it comes to picking an advisor, because they have life and market experience.
4. Work with a team as opposed to one person. I find that advisors that are part of a team have more bandwidth and internal support to give you the time and attention you need and deserve.
5. Check an advisor's U4, which shows their employment history and any complaints, lawsuits, or judgments they have against them (among other things).
6. Check how many firms the advisor has been with. If an advisor has been employed by three different firms in the past five years, this is not a good sign. Advisors typically change firms because they are getting a large check to make the move. Longevity with one or two firms demonstrates stability. You don't want to move your accounts every couple years to follow an advisor who is mostly concerned about their own paycheck.
7. Have an in-person conversation where you meet your advisor face to face. It is always surprising to

me how many clients have never met their advisor in person. If an in-person meeting is not possible because of your geographic locations, then meet via Skype or FaceTime. In my opinion, you should look your advisor in the eyes when you establish your relationship.

8. Get a feeling for how pushy they are…you want someone who will respect your comfort level and risk tolerance as opposed to forcing you into an investment you are not comfortable with.

9. After you establish a relationship with your advisor, it is important to meet with him or her on a quarterly, semi-annual, or annual basis to review your financial plan. Based on your performance and changing life circumstances, your advisor should evaluate how you are doing relative to your long-term goals.

10. Consider their financial interests and potential bias. At some brokerages, advisors are rewarded for selling particular products. You want an advisor who gives impartial and unbiased advice. Their advice should only be based on their years of experience and knowledge.

11. Ask an advisor how they get compensated. Confirm whether they get paid by commission, an

Appendix

annual fee, or some other way. Ask the advisor to put any fees in writing, and keep this document so you can refer to it in the future.

12. A common scenario is that clients will have their assets held at multiple financial institutions. Typically, I recommend people *consider* consolidating their accounts with one advisor. It was common in our parents' generation to spread investment accounts among different firms to achieve diversification and reduce risk. Now, it can be more beneficial to have all your assets managed in one place for economies of scale in pricing and a holistic view of your net worth and how it is tracking relative to your long-term goals.

13. In the event that you decide to spread your accounts at different firms, or if for some reason all your accounts cannot be consolidated (like a 401k or 529 account), make sure that your main advisor is reviewing ALL your accounts as one complete whole. This is important for asset allocation, account titles, beneficiary designations, and investment performance. You will then have a 360-degree view of your total performance, which will help you track if you are on the right path.

14. There are different terms used for financial advisors. Frequently used terms are wealth manager, financial planner, broker, investment advisor, financial consultant, or registered representative, among others. Some titles are purely for marketing purposes, and some have legal and regulatory meaning. Be sure to ask your advisor what credentials they have (e.g., Series 7, Series 65, CFP, MBA, etc.), what they mean, and how these credentials will benefit you as their client.

15. If you decide to switch from one advisor to another, make sure you are aware of any hidden costs associated with the move. For example, if the new advisor cannot hold one of your investments, he or she might need to sell it. This sale could trigger recognition of capital gains or some kind of penalty charge. You do not want to be surprised by a higher tax bill or loss of return because you paid a surrender charge to move your account. You want complete transparency with how a move will impact your investments, fees, and any taxes. This way, you are making an informed decision.

Appendix

IV. When to Hire a Financial Advisor

In my experience, a trusted financial advisor is a key partner in times of transition. They can be especially helpful during life events, when you are:

- recently separated or divorced,
- about to have children,
- recently engaged or married, or
- newly widowed.

They are also invaluable when you are:

- selling a business,
- exercising stock options,
- selling or buying real property, or
- receiving an inheritance.

V. Five Reasons It Might Be Time to Change Financial Advisors

1. If you have been with a financial advisor for years and they have never done a financial plan for you.
2. If your advisor is not giving you guidance on all your accounts (ones held at their firm and ones held at other financial institutions), you should question why. Remember that you want a holistic view of how all your assets and accounts are performing relative to your goals.

3. If your advisor has never asked about your family or how you want to transfer your wealth to your family, this is not good. Estate planning is an integral component of your financial plan and should not be overlooked.
4. If you feel like you cannot open up to your advisor or are uncomfortable asking questions, this is a bad sign. You need to work with someone that makes you feel comfortable, treats you with respect, and encourages you to ask questions.
5. If your advisor is not meeting with you on a regular basis to review your performance and how you are tracking toward your financial planning goals, it might be time to switch to an advisor who conducts performance reviews as an integral part of their service model.

One More Thing!

How to Be Your Own Handywoman

Another category Scott excelled in was taking care of our house maintenance. He scheduled when to change smoke detector batteries, knew how to shut off a gushing water pipe, troubleshot our HVAC system, switched out air filters, and a multitude of other maintenance items. I knew none of this but, out of fear, was determined to get a handle on it.

The contractor who built our house agreed to come over and be my house maintenance guide. Together, we walked through the house, and I made a list of all the things I had to track. I learned a lot about ongoing maintenance, especially the importance of changing air filters on a regular basis. From this list, I made a spreadsheet of what needed to be done each month. I also made sure I knew the contact information for our plumber, lawn service, HVAC technician, and general handyman. I called each of them to make sure they were still in business and able to come to our house in case of an emergency. I learned to do things myself and made several trips to Home Depot to get supplies.

This knowledge has helped me over the years, and I now know to ask lots of questions whenever we have a plumbing, heating, cooling, or maintenance issue. I take notes and pictures in my phone so I can refer to them if the same problem occurs again. Being intelligent and self-sufficient when it comes to house maintenance is a confidence booster, and I highly recommend taking on the challenge or at least being more inquisitive. You never know when your knowledge might come in handy!

NOTES

www.ingramcontent.com/pod-product-compliance
Lightning Source LLC
Chambersburg PA
CBHW051357290426
44108CB00015B/2058